DATA ENGINEERING

A Novel Approach to Data Design

first edition

The story of an old man and his young son who struggle to narrow their generational gap. The gap begins to close when Dad cuts off Luke's allowance funds and requires Luke to work for his money. Dad helps Luke form a business and Dad uses data modeling, value chain and team dynamics to bridge the generational divide. Luke learns about both information management and human behavior.

BRIAN SHIVE

Published by:
Technics Publications, LLC
2 Lindsley Road
Basking Ridge, NJ 07920 U.S.A.

http://www.TechnicsPub.com

Edited by Carol Lehn
Cover design by Mark Brye

ISBN, print ed.   978-1-935504-60-3
ISBN, Kindle ed.   978-1-935504-61-0
ISBN, ePub ed.   978-1-935504-62-7

First Printing 2013

Library of Congress Control Number: 2013948311

ATTENTION SCHOOLS AND BUSINESSES: Technics Publications books are available at quantity discounts with bulk purchase for educational, business, or sales promotional use. For information, please email Steve Hoberman, President of Technics Publications, at me@stevehoberman.com.

Contents

Preface

This book is aimed at IT professionals or curious adults who wish to learn about the foundational concepts that can increase the likelihood for IT project success. These concepts were commonly used and were highly successful at IBM in the 1960s and 1970s. These concepts have morphed over the decades as thousands of organizations and people outside of IBM began to use them. My personal and subjective observation is that these foundational concepts are not utilized sufficiently today. This book is intended to broadly communicate the concepts to the best of my recollection. To the extent IT projects deviate from these concepts, they under-deliver, overcharge, are late, or flat out fail.

Foundational Concepts

The three foundational concepts in data engineering are data models, value chain models, and team dynamics. Data models define the meaning or semantics of the "things of interest" to the enterprise. Value chain models define the flow of "things of interest" from external actors into the processes of the enterprise, define how the processes add value to the "things of interest", and define how the completed "things of interest" are passed to external actors as finished goods or services. Team dynamics means that people need to be conscious of their behavior and how it impacts the ability of the team to deliver value successfully. People need to be aware of the uniqueness of each individual, as well as how we are all members of the same enterprise.

Your IT project is very likely to succeed if you are clear on data and process, as well as maintaining constructive interpersonal relationships. Also, data and process exist with different viewpoints defined by different audiences and purposes. I learned these data and process concepts from John Zachman and Ted Codd at IBM in the late 1970s. The interpersonal relationship ideas have evolved from my own circuitous journey of trial and error over many decades. I present this trio of concepts by using stories from my life, in hopes of ease of consumption, breadth of audience, and clarity through example.

Data Modeling Ideals versus Reality

Data modeling cannot be effective as an independent design artifact. Consistent success with data modeling requires a related value chain and constructive team dynamics.

This book will describe three important data modeling artifacts called the Conceptual Data Model (CDM), the Logical Data Model (LDM), and the Physical Data Model (PDM). These three types of models will be described as idealized concepts in their pure form. This is similar to Platonic idealism, the archetypes that describe the perfect form of a thing while recognizing that the real world is built of things that always vary from the ideal. The value of these three ideal concepts is that we can take a data model and categorize which portions of it align with each concept.

Of course, when I sit down to do a CDM for my shipping department I hope to align perfectly with the CDM ideal for the entire modeling effort. The reality is that I have rarely achieved this ideal due to time, lack of access to experts, complexity of the problem, or my personal defects. When time or budget expire on the shipping department CDM effort, my team sits down and discusses which portions of the CDM are true and which portions are leaning towards LDM or PDM. We probably won't be able to fix the errors, but we can all use the shipping department CDM model with full consensus and awareness of the imperfections. We can compensate for CDM weaknesses as we do the LDM and PDM.

Agreeing on where the imperfections exist and how they vary from the ideal provides a surprising degree of value as the project moves beyond data modeling and into design and coding.

Process Modeling Value Chains

Each data model will have a corresponding value chain model. All of the inputs and outputs in the value chain will be represented in the data model. A value chain is a set of processes that take low value things and transform them into high value things. Value is defined in the context of your customers. If my customers are hungry carnivores, then hamburgers have value to my customer. If, on the other hand, my customers are hungry vegetarians, then salads would be of more value than hamburgers. Value chains exist within a single business but can also exist across multiple businesses. Each step in a value chain represents a specialization in the division of labor. Specializations can be outsourced or in-sourced to optimize profitability.

Brains and Behavior

We will touch upon some ancient wisdom on human behavior, as well as some contemporary brain research, to present ideas on how we can behave to optimize collaboration, efficiency, and the probability of IT project success.

Chapter 1
A Data Modeling Story

It was another dreary, rainy day, and the bad news seemed to be coming in waves.

Yet another IT project had been cancelled. Now we were having the project postmortem to assign blame and begin the process of punishing the guilty. My boss was visibly sweating as he tried to defend our data model and database design. His peers were jointly attacking like hyenas swarming on a weakened gazelle.

Just as the walls of his last defense were beginning to be breached, I felt a buzzing in my pocket from a poorly timed cell phone call. I checked the caller Id to find it was my mom. She only calls during work hours when it is critically important, so I slipped out of the conference room to take the call in the hallway.

It was an emergency room doctor calling to tell me my mom was having severe chest pains and was undergoing a series of tests. I said I would be right there and returned to the conference room to excuse myself. As I opened the door, the corporate Vice President started asking me leading questions. As the focus of questioning migrated back to my boss, I was thinking about all the love and effort my mom invested in my upbringing. Suddenly, my life looked like an emergency room triage process where priorities are set and action is taken, immediately. I abruptly interrupted the Vice President, announced my mother's condition, and then exited while the Vice President was trying to ask me "just one last question."

As I arrived at the hospital, nurses were adding some pain medication to her IV solution. The tension in her face visibly relaxed as the drugs began to work. The doctor arrived just moments later to tell us that she had not had a heart attack. Her face relaxed another level, returning to her normal demeanor. While we were waiting to check out of the hospital, she asked me to turn on the TV. A documentary was on PBS about the Dust Bowl. Mom had lived through the Dust Bowl as a child in Kansas. When she sees things from the past, they trigger memories and storytelling. She told me this story:

Brian, when our ancestors first came to the plains of Kansas, the grass was eight feet tall. In order to see across the Great Plains, you had to sit on a large horse, and even then, the grass was still shoulder high. Our family had 250 acres of prime land acquired under the Homestead Act, but we could farm only a small section of it due to the prairie grass. When the tractor was invented, we bought one and started to plow up the entire acreage. In the first two years, we paid off all our debts and were positioned to be millionaires in about four more years.

The neighboring Native Americans would stop us on the road and warn us that if we kept plowing under the native grass, the Spirit of the Earth would become unbalanced. They said we would come to regret the tractor that seemed like such a good thing to us at the time.

Our family was mostly of German and Irish descent, and our cultural traditions did not recognize the Spirit of the Earth as an entity of significance. Grandpa Kappelman got the family together to discuss this environmental issue relative to the financial bonanza that our new tractors were uncovering. Of course the vote was a landslide for riches, with only a single vote cast for preservation of the environment. Aunt Ida, the lone dissenter, talked to animals and trees, and she insisted her talking was a dialog. Her lone irrational vote was considered typical for naive Ida.

The Kiowa tribe had warned the technologically advanced white tribe, but the warnings were almost universally ignored. All our neighbors got tractors, and for the next harvest season the riches flowed like a flooding Texas river in springtime.

That October, the Kiowa tribe was exiled to a reservation in Texas with no grass, no trees, and no wildlife. There was a brief article on page nine of the local paper, and people discussed the issue for a couple of days. We felt safer now that they were gone. We were also certain that we were superior to the primitive tribes who did not understand our technology and our advanced civilizations.

The true wisdom of the Kiowa began to germinate in our minds when, in the next year, there was no rain and the wind blew day and night for weeks at a time. We got no rain for six years, and of course the crops all died, as did the children of Kansas by the thousands. Breathing in dust becomes impossible to avoid when a cloud of it blows across the barren plains, 20,000 feet tall moving at 50 miles an hour. Children seemed to be particularly susceptible to death from dust pneumonia. So the Kiowa nation, who had the wisdom to understand the environment, was banished to obscurity. And we, the advanced civilization, stood starving and dying by the thousands.

Our family, with one exception, believed that our farming and plowing actions did not cause the Dust Bowl. They asserted that it was just a quirk of nature, soon to pass. Further, we believed—minus one vote—that the Spirit of the Earth was not out of balance, and we thought the rains and big profits would return any day now.

Well, after a decade of drought, the rains returned and a new crop was sprouting into a certain bumper crop. Ida was surprised that the Spirit of the Earth was back in balance so quickly. Half way through the growing season, a cloud of grasshoppers swarmed through the farm and ate every living plant in sight over the course of a week. The grasshoppers blocked out the sun to the point where you needed to turn on a light to read in the house at noon on a clear day. With Biblical catastrophes popping up repeatedly, the Kiowa leader returned to town and repeated his warning about the glossy shine of wealth and the subtle and hidden virtues of harmony with nature.

Grandpa Kappelman reconvened the family elders for a vote on moving to California. Ida insisted that we start with a vote on the issue of the Spirit of the Earth being out of balance. The German pride in the room blocked this vote, but the undercurrent of contrition was palpable a mile away. The vote was to stay in Kansas and accept responsibility for our role in inflicting environmental damage. The Federal farming practices to preserve the soil were adopted completely. In time, the Spirit of the Earth would be healed enough to support farming.

So the lesson here is that the web of environmental dependencies is easy to ignore, while the lure of wealth and power is hard to ignore.

This seemed to be my day to learn about setting priorities for broad, long-term objectives. We checked out of the hospital looking forward to returning home. When we got home, my son Luke was playing a computer game. He did not look up to greet us. Rather, he waved briefly and then returned to the slaughter. I am having difficulties understanding Luke and his enigmatic generation.

Luke is 9 years old, and I, his 62-year-old father, cannot keep up with all the games, gadgets, movies, and lingo. In some aspects, I see Luke's generation surpassing mine, while in other ways I see the opposite to be true. My generation was shaped by non-electronic games and gadgets, where the electronic aspects of games and gadgets were generated by our neurons, no batteries required. We were required to use our imaginations in our play, and we were encouraged to construct our own gadgets.

Luke gets his games and gadgets in packages that say "batteries required." He just follows the pathways available in the package. Granted, the graphics are great and the excitement is high, but there is still a loss of creativity. My generation was raised and shaped by a community of positive and constructive (non-zero sum) social bonds. These bonds came from social groups such as family, church, neighborhood, scouting, sports, band—institutions that model community.

Growing and learning from face-to-face social interactions in a positive social environment builds critical interpersonal strengths such as listening, humility, team behavior, compromise, and leadership. Luke's social interactions are increasingly migrating from face to face and becoming gadget to gadget. The contents, integrity, and veracity of his social bonds decline as he migrates to non-face-to-face electronic social interactions. Too many action-oriented video games targeted at males portray our world today as being mostly a zero-sum affair in which, for every winner, there's a loser. The reality is that we should be teaching young males to seek non-zero sum relationships; when presented with an adversary. Luke's gadgets promote the opposite.

While recognizing that Luke's generation outstrips mine in a dozen ways, I finally put my foot down and demanded that he spend some time operating back in my old-fashioned times. Luke will now earn his toy money with a job. Yes, that word actually was "J-O-B." That word means you are working and getting paid by the customer—not by dad.

We have 17 acres containing several groves of lemon trees. My brother has been harvesting them for 47 years; he recently moved to a retirement home. Now Luke is getting to be the boss of his new lemon business. Luke will get to express his creativity in the lemon business (or get no toys), and he will do so with customers and partners who require constructive social interactions for all parties to be satisfied in the arrangement.

Value Chains and Data Models

Luke was fairly stunned to realize that "good old dad" was actually going to stop buying toys and make his summer job the single source of money for his acquisition of new things. When the implications of this sudden and sweeping change were fully grasped, Luke asked me, "How do I run a lemon business?" I told him that he—himself, by himself—would have to answer this question for the first season. After that, I would assist him more and more each season by giving him business tips and a computing system to manage his business. For the first season, the only advice I would be giving Luke were the paradigms called *value chain* and *data modeling*. Value chain is the collection of processes that a business uses to convert raw materials into finished goods. Data modeling is the specification of the things of interest to a business.

I knew that this vision of how businesses (and the entire world) operate would fall on deaf ears, but planting this foundational seed in the back of his mind would bear fruit in his teen years, just as he was teetering between self-indulgent lethargy and self-sacrificing hard work. Luke's business experiences would someday keep the teenage Luke on the path of progress. And sure enough, Luke half listened to and half responded to my lecture. Over the coming lemon seasons, my prediction of the benefits of these paradigms became increasingly true as his mental investment in "value chain" and "data modeling" rapidly became the key paradigms driving his business model evolution.

I chose to give Luke his introduction to value chain during a winter snow storm after the electricity went out. We were hovering near the fireplace when I said, "Lukas," his formal name, which engendered fear and rapt attention, "it is time for your first business lesson. Put your cell phone game down and listen, please." He pleaded again for clemency and a reprieve from his financial circumstance, but I denied his appeal and proceeded with his opening business lesson. "Luke, do you remember that year when dad took medical leave from work for a few months?" He, of course, easily recalled it, since it was the first time he fully bonded with his newly adopted dad.

I had had a stroke and cancer and spent months on leave with Luke, who was three at the time. We would get up early in the morning and walk the trails of our 17 acres to observe and revel in nature's displays. Playing with a three-year-old boy surrounded by nature was a far cry from my adult urban corporate environment, where I suspect that my health condition had germinated. I had my triage priorities set on corporate success, and I forgot about the joy of a child playing in the forest. The good part about a stroke and cancer is that you get your triage meter adjusted big time. Taking the time to play with your three-year-old son in the forest all day, while feeling eternity's hand on your shoulder, was both healing and scary.

Early one fall morning, we were walking the trails in deep fog when the sun suddenly poked her fingers of light out between the lifting veils of fog. As we rounded a corner in the trail, there were a dozen spider webs on one large tree, with fog-dew-drops on every strand. Each intersection of strands contained a glistening crystal. The light was hitting the drops in a way that made them seem to be self-luminous. This light show ebbed and flowed with the patterns of lifting fog. As we watched, a fly crashed into one web and struggled to escape. With each struggle, the web flexed and the light from the dew drops danced in tune with the undulating fly. Then, the branch holding the upper part of the web started to shake from the struggle below. This branch, in turn, shook its neighbor's branch which, in turn, shook the web of the neighboring spider. Now both webs were dancing out of phase to the same struggle, and instantly the light show doubled in size and intensity. The neighboring spider ran out from his watch station and looked for the source of the ruckus. After a complete scan of his web, he—undoubtedly dejectedly—returned empty handed.

After reminiscing about that morning, I told Luke that value chains and spider webs are similar things. The spider web tells the spider about all of the action within his sphere of control. In a similar way, you will have a sphere of control in your summer lemon business. This sphere of control will be defined and managed by your value chain and your data model. These two ideas will be the keys to how you manage, evolve, and profit from your business. Additionally, you will need to interact with the value chains of your partners and customers. Your web will touch your neighbor's webs. This interaction should produce a win-win relationship across all parties or else your business will fail. These win/win, or non-zero sum, relationships are critical to your lemon business's success. There will be times when you are having problems with employees, customers, and partners in your business. You will either find a win/win solution or your business will suffer. Finding a win/win solution is more likely when value chain and data models are the paradigms that shape your thinking. Also, when you use the paradigms of value chain and data modeling to design your business, guide the execution of your business, and measure your business, you will be more likely to increase your profits. Upon hearing "increase your profits," the gaze of glaze finally fully evaporated from Luke's face and a look of rapt attention with ears wide open suddenly appeared.

Value Chain Analogies

So an analogy would be if my web is my value chain, and if your web is your value chain, and if the tree branches are the agents that tie our value chains together, then there is a higher value chain that is the union of our value chains.

Another analogy using the dust bowl example is if the Earth's environmental ecosphere is a value chain, and if the world's economy is a value chain, and if the environment impacts the economy, and if the economy impacts the environment, then there is a higher value chain that is the union of the two value chains.

Ultimately, the union of all interdependent value chains is the real world that we experience every day. This invisible set of cause-and-effect links must be clearly understood to be successful in business, environmental science, economics, and just about any endeavor. Information systems (such as brains and computers) view subsets of the real world value chains, since information systems are limited in their capacity and resources.

The models below from Luke's lemonade business have some separate things (boxes) and have some interdependent things (lines between boxes). These models are purposely small so that the principle of separate things being interwoven can be seen. These diagrams are presented later in a more readable form as they are built through the chapters that follow.

Data Model

Value Chain Model

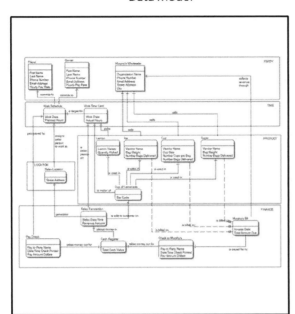
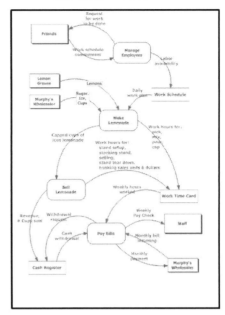

To further demonstrate interdependence in this simple lemonade business, I will add some dependencies between the data model and the value chain model, shown on the next page with the dashed lines.

Data Model

Value Chain Model

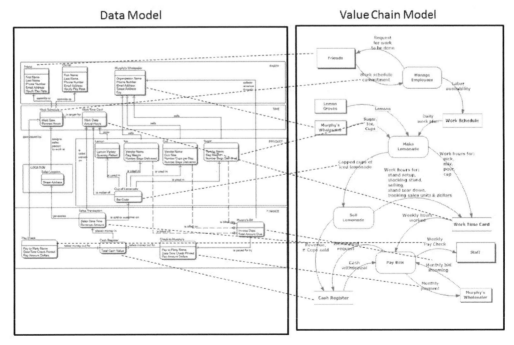

Businesses and computer systems consist of things all woven together into a web by a particular configuration of relationships.

Hopefully the things and relationships in our models match the real world things and relationships of our business. Also, we hope that the things and relationships of our models are faithfully built into our information systems. If so, the business will get maximum value from their investment in computing capability.

Key Points

- We tend to see the differences between things; only secondarily do we consider the interdependencies between things.

- We tend to overlook the degree to which things are highly interdependent.

- Value chain and data models clearly depict how our "separate things" are actually completely "interdependent things."

Each value chain has a design that represents the structure, the plan, and the hopes for the value chain. This design will be documented in Product and Service Master Data, which we will discuss in detail later. As the value chain executes through actions and transactions, the design becomes manifest in the real world. Value chain execution requires business process instructions for both the people in the business and the machines (software instructions).

These actions and transactions have a data model corollary called transactional data, which we will discuss later. These actions and transactions generate a historical record of instances of the value chain lifecycle. Real world value chain actions and transactions can vary from their design due to real world complexity and exceptions not anticipated in the value chain design.

Lastly, the measurement of value chain transactions requires us to have a metrics generation process that captures master and transactional data and then transforms them into a schema that allows us to measure the value chain. These metrics show where strengths and weaknesses exist in the business and provide feedback on the wisdom of your business models, value chains, and data models.

The benefits of the value chain design are greatly enhanced when the value chain design is stored on a computer. Value chain designs stored on a computer can:

- Run simulations to guide the business owner as to the profitability and risks associated with proposed alternative approaches to the current value chains (called *business simulation*)
- Take business volume forecasts and drive the scheduling and ordering of resources required to meet these volumes (called *enterprise resource planning*)
- Inform and train all participants as to the roles and positions they play in delivering value to the end customer
- Train employees and partners
- Calculate performance bonuses for value chain leaders

Luke asked several questions that proved I was failing to be clear. Also, he had been squirming around in his chair and looking out the window, so I tried a new approach. Luke and I had recently toured the Boeing airplane factory near my house. He was totally engrossed with the process and the potential outcome (flying to Hawaii). I shifted my presentation from professorial axioms that bolstered my already overinflated confidence to present a single concrete example from our tour of Boeing. Designing and building airplanes involves the engineering value chain. We start with designs, build instances of designs, and then measure the instances to see if they match the designs within our tolerances.

Designs for Airplanes

Design	Construction	Testing

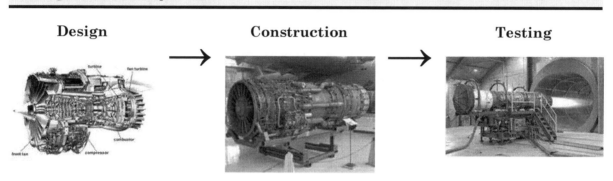

In data modeling, the master data for products and services represents the designs of the things the business will deliver to customers. The actual constructed engine represents the execution of the design for the engine. In data modeling, transactional data will represent the execution of our designs. The measurement state of the engine is represented by the testing and quality assurance of the engine. Installing instruments to measure vibration, thrust, and pollutants is the measurement state of the engine. If some engines are generating insufficient thrust, the design of the engines will need to be changed. New engines must be built and the thrust re-measured. In data modeling, our measurement will appear in dimensional modeling, which will drive our reporting data warehouse.

VALUE CHAIN COMPONENTS
All value chains are represented by four simple components:

- External Actors (rectangle)
- Input Flows (arrow coming into a process)
- Processes (box with rounded corners)
- Output Flows (arrow coming out of a process)

The diagram on the facing page is a simple value chain represented by a data flow diagram. Further, these components can be nested within themselves to decompose the value chain into more and more detailed descriptions of process and data flows between processes.

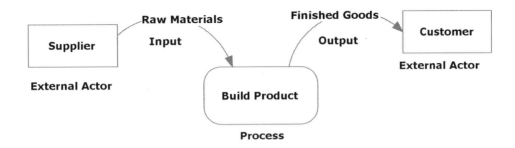

DATA MODEL COMPONENTS

All data models are represented using three simple components:

- Entities and Relationships (boxes are the nouns and lines are the verbs)
- Uniqueness Constraints (primary key and alternate keys)
- Attributes (properties for each box)

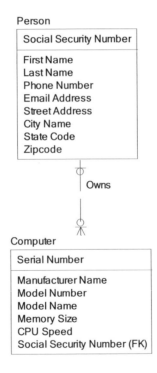

I told Luke that the clarity, consistency, and universal applicability of value chain and data model thinking will drive thousands of dollars into his pocket—if he can learn these simple and powerful ideas. Again Luke was listening—looking, leaning forward, and almost tasting the monetary fruits that could come from his impending lemon business.

He asked how much Uncle Bill made last season, and I replied, "About $4,700 of profit. But Uncle Bill had disease in many of the trees last year. Uncle Bill sprayed late last

September, and this year every tree should be more productive." With curiosity in his eyes, Luke asked "Tell me more about this value chain thing."

Value chain is a sequence of activities that produce a series of results that eventually lead to the delivery of finished goods to the customer, resulting in profits for your pocket. This linkage of "processes/activities" and "artifacts/results" is specifically designed to allow for specialization in the division of labor and to articulate the artifacts or things that flow between specializations.

Each activity represents a specific skill required to deliver the finished goods. Each skill takes some input artifacts having small value and then executes the skill of the specialization, delivering output artifacts containing greater value. For example, if my specialization is to be a farmer of wheat, and your specialization is to be a grinder of wheat to produce flour, then my value chain output of "wheat" is your value chain input.

The artifacts in the value chain will be defined in a data model, and this data model will drive the structure and contents of your computing system database. The structure and contents of your computing system database are the limiting factor for the set of capabilities the system can deliver to its users, so your database foundation has to be right.

Key Points

- To increase our odds of being successful in business and information technology, we need to think of the world as consisting of:
  - Designs: The ideas that describe what we hope to build or deliver (Master Data).
  - Execution: The manifestation of our designs into real world deliverables (Transactional Data).
  - Measurement: The metrics that tell us if our real world deliverables live up to our designs, and if our customers are getting value from our deliverables (Business Intelligence Data).

- It is critical that the pattern of things and their relationships for the real world business and the patterns in the computer system are aligned.

- These similarities are easier to achieve when you use value chain and data models as your method of thinking, communicating, and interacting with computing systems.

The Burger Bun Conceptual Value Chain and Data Model

Luke had lapsed back into fidgeting, complaining, and looking out the window. The biggest complaint was hunger, which was reasonable considering we were two hours late getting lunch. Luke loves the local hamburger stand, so we went there for lunch. I got a drab salad, conforming to my new diet, and Luke had two mini-burgers and a milkshake.

When we returned, I tried the Boeing trick of moving my teaching style from philosophical to a more tangible, real, and high priority subject like...burgers. "Luke, let's take an example value chain and call it the 'Burger Bun Value Chain.'" Luke, however, was stuffed with fat and protein. He was sleepy and had lost interest in the burger topic. Next time, I vowed to present this value chain example to hungry, awake students, but for now I forced Luke to listen. Below are some specializations in this value chain:

- Granger: A business that sells bags of wheat seed
- Farmer: A business that plants seeds to grow wheat
- Miller: A business that grinds wheat to make flour
- Baker: A business that uses flour to make buns
- Burger Stand: A portable business that uses buns to make hamburgers

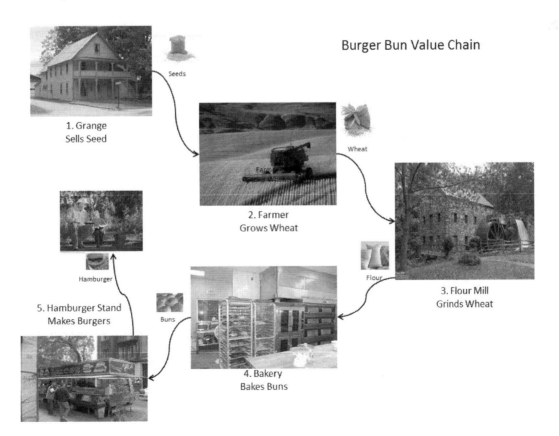

Burger Bun Value Chain

1. Grange
Sells Seed

2. Farmer
Grows Wheat

3. Flour Mill
Grinds Wheat

4. Bakery
Bakes Buns

5. Hamburger Stand
Makes Burgers

Seeds

Wheat

Flour

Buns

Hamburger

Each specialization in the burger bun value chain performs a set of activities. They each take artifacts from upstream, apply their unique skill to convert them into new and more valuable artifacts, and then pass them downstream in the value chain. At this point Luke jumped in to ask why we were not talking about lemons. He was sad to hear that he would learn the principles of business before he would learn to apply them with his unique and memorable style of trial and error.

Value chain involves many "things," or "artifacts," that are referred to by nouns in our language. The data model will specify those "things" that play a critical role in each value chain so that we can speak and think clearly about them and understand the relationships between them. Following is a diagram of the ordering and delivery of products part of a simple hamburger bun value chain, along with its related data model. Marketing, sales, contracts, billing, and payments are not covered.

The facing page contains two diagrams. This value chain model is expressed as a Data Flow Diagram, or DFD. The DFD shows how input entities are converted to become output entities, and it shows how different external actors can interact. For example, Luke wanted to play the role of a farm owner, and he wanted me to be the mill owner. In the DFD below, the mill owner, Dad, places an order for 40 bags of wheat grain with the farm owner, Luke. Luke checks Dad's credit rating and payment history and decides that I am a low-risk customer. He approves my order for 40 bags of wheat grain. Inside of Luke's process called "Manage Farm," Luke bags up 40 bags of wheat grain, puts them on a truck, and delivers them to my milling facility. This is the arrow on the right side of the DFD going between "Manage Farm" and "Manage Mill." The arrow is labeled "Wheat Grain" which, in this instance, represents 40 bags of wheat grain flowing from the farm to the mill.

Trudy, our neighbor and best friend, walked in for the last part of our discussion and looked perplexed. I asked Luke to summarize our lesson to test his grasp of the value chain topic. Luke told Trudy that things with a small amount of value, like a stalk of wheat, can be turned into things with a large amount of value, like a hamburger bun, by moving these things through the steps of a value chain. The value chain is a collection of specialists who collaborate to deliver value to a customer. Trudy and I raised our eyebrows and crooked our heads in approval and disbelief. Luke got it completely!

Next to the value chain model on the facing page is a conceptual data model of the things of interest to the business owners of the Hamburger Bun Value Chain. For example, if Luke is the owner of a farm and I am the owner of a mill, the CDM shows how my things are related to Luke's things. Luke's farm gets an order for wheat grain from dad's mill.

Value Chain

Data Model

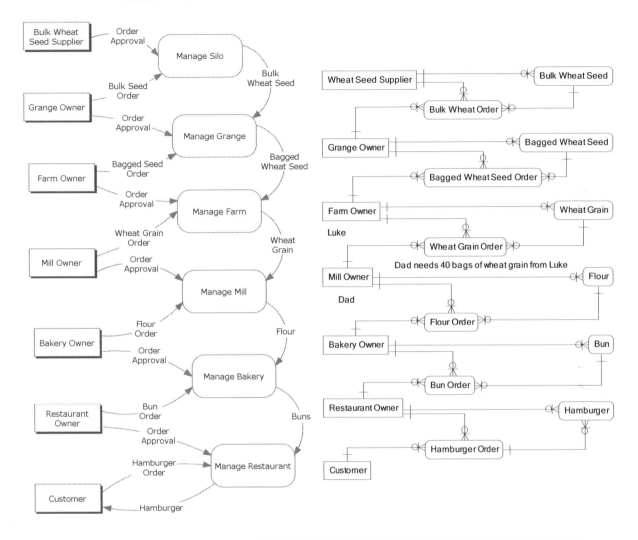

Key Points

- Humans dominate the earth partially because our brains, cultures, and information systems facilitate collaboration between specializations called value chains.

- Collaborations between specializations can be chained together into larger and larger webs, resulting in prosperity for all participants.

- Human value chains can span the planet. They can merge and split to form optimal configurations, given environmental demands.

Chapter 3
The Value Chain for Designing and Building, Called Engineering

We took a couple of weeks away from our business training since Luke was busy with school work and had suffered a cold and a mild bout with the flu bug. As he regained his health and acquired a chunk of free time, we returned to our preparation for his summer lemon business.

My next educational objective was to illustrate how value chains and data models can be designed with systematic discipline while still allowing for huge creativity and expressiveness. My 34 years of IT work are laced with ad hoc, extemporaneous improvisations that tried to reinvent value chain and data modeling.

Highly intelligent computing professionals can tend to acquire a case of overconfidence. This leads them to ignore the structure and discipline of their own industry and launch off down some appealing and creative, but damaging, pathways. Additionally, industry data models and pattern libraries are often underused for the same "not invented here" syndrome. I caught this affliction for decades, but I wanted Luke to respect the past century of engineering discipline and not lapse into thinking he is smarter than the cumulative wisdom of thousands of his predecessors.

To make this point, I started shopping around for engineering projects we could visit, but first Luke hopped online to read a quick definition from Wikipedia:

> ***Engineering*** *is the discipline, art, skill, profession, and technology of acquiring and applying scientific, mathematical, economic, social, and practical knowledge, in order to design and build structures, machines, devices, systems, materials and processes.*

I would add that engineering design generally solves the design problem from general to specific. This is called *forward engineering*. In some cases, you have an existing product where you need to *reverse engineer* the design. Reverse engineering goes from specific to general. Engineering also ensures that the general design is faithfully embodied in the specific design. Of course, the specific design adds some new aspects to the general design while being faithful to the general design's intent.

The Value Chain for House Designing

I have a friend, Ray, who is a structural engineer. He designs and builds houses, and he suggested I let Luke observe his next project. At first, this seemed like a waste of time, but Ray pointed out that houses are concrete things that are easily understood. Also, housing has a long history of treating engineering as a discipline. Therefore, if Luke can understand the process of designing houses, he can be both structured and creative in designing various products that need lemons.

I was doubtful that Luke would benefit, but since I was curious myself how the process worked, I said yes. Luke was resistant to the idea, but he likes Ray's wacky sense of humor, so he said, "Sure, let's go; that Ray is a real kick in the pants."

Ray started with a discussion of the steps in his process, shown in the table below from general on top to specific on the bottom.

Ray's House Project
Scope
Owner's View
Architect's View
Builder's View
Subcontractor's View
Finished House

He starts out with a general scope statement for the project. This is the most general state of Ray's design. Then he adds enough details in the owner's view step to get clear agreement with the customer on a cost and timeframe for the project. Ray uses a cardboard house to give the owner something concrete to look at. Next, he sits at his computer and works with 3-D geometry to design the architect's view. This view describes internal structure that was not relevant to the owner's view. Ray's builder, who will do the actual work of construction, will take Ray's blueprints, partition them for each subcontractor, and then add some details to produce the builder's view. Ray's builder subcontracts most of the labor to specialists in plumbing, electrical, sheet rock, framing, etc. The subcontractors will add material suppliers and specific SKUs to the builder's view to create the subcontractor's view. When the project is complete, the family will move into their "finished house."

LEVEL 1 – DEFINING THE SCOPE

First, we watched Ray talk with the Smith family as they discussed what they wanted in their new house. The husband wanted a pool and a workshop, the wife wanted a 1,500 square foot kitchen, and the kids wanted a media room that sounded a lot like

Disneyland. Luke viewed the parents as being unreasonable, while he found the kids' needs for their Disneyland media room to be perfectly rational.

Ray locked the Smiths in on a budget and then gradually established priorities for allocation of the budget. Everyone was partially disappointed in the end, but the final compromise was true to the budget and priorities. The purpose of defining the Level 1 deliverable of scope was to ensure the price and features of the house meet the new owner's general needs and are within his budget.

LEVEL 2 – DESIGNING THE OWNER'S VIEW

Next, Ray built a 3-D computer model of the house and a miniature cardboard house with little trees and fake grass. The cardboard house had a roof that could be removed, making the interior rooms easily visible. In the 3-D computer model house, they could walk through the rooms and look around. Ray sat down with the Smith family and walked them through both the cardboard house and the 3-D model house. Each family member had some comments on likes and dislikes.

Ray updated the two model houses with the changes requested by the Smiths, updated the cost and time estimates, and then repeated the process. After the second review with the Smiths, everyone agreed to the price, time, and features of the new house. Their previous disappointment had now turned to excitement about the prospects of a new house. The purpose of the Level 2 deliverable for the owner's view was to add enough details to the scope statement to ensure the owner fully understood what he would be getting for his money.

LEVEL 3 – DESIGNING THE ARCHITECT'S VIEW

A few weeks later, Ray invited us over to see the architectural blueprints he had drafted. They were huge sheets of paper with front views, side views, top views, and landscape views. The Level 3 deliverable of the architect's view was created in part to communicate to the Smith family, but it was mostly created to communicate to Jones & Sons Contractors, who would be the builders for this project. They needed a clear and detailed picture of what they were going to build.

LEVEL 4 – DESIGNING THE BUILDER'S VIEW

About a month later, we got a call from Jones & Sons Contractors to come over and see the builder's blueprints. This time there were many more large rolls of blueprints. Jones had a set of blueprints for each subcontractor who would be working on the house. There were separate blueprints for foundation, framing, plumbing, wiring, flooring, and several others we chose not to view. Luke noticed that Ray had called for a metal I-beam in the large open space, but Jones' blueprints had called for a glue-laminated beam in place of the I-beam. Jones explained that the I-beam manufacturers were all on strike, so the cost and time for them would be prohibitive. He had substituted a glue-laminated beam since they are half the cost and can be picked up at any time.

Jones explained that this Level 4 deliverable of the builder's view was created to communicate clearly to the subcontractors exactly what materials they should use when they start working. The subcontractors would be the people who would pick up the materials, take them to the site, and assemble the materials to create the house.

LEVEL 5 – DESIGNING THE SUB-CONTRACTOR'S VIEW

Shortly after visiting Jones, we got a call from John at Valley Framing subcontractors. John invited us over to see what he had created using Jones' blueprints. John had long lists of materials, with quantities for each item and the supplier addresses where the items could be picked up. This was the most detailed description of a house I have ever seen. He had pictures of nailing patterns to use at key stress points, as well as the fabrication sequence for the roof joists. John explained that this Level 5 deliverable of the subcontractor's view was to communicate to the people who would pick up all the materials, transport them to the site, and swing the hammers that built the house.

LEVEL 6 – APPRECIATING THE FINISHED HOUSE

Ray called us about four months later to visit the finished house. The inspectors were there at the time, doing the last inspections before issuing the occupancy permit for the new owners. Luke was very impressed with the final result; having seen the process from inception to completion made it even more memorable for him. The purpose of the Level 6 deliverable was to give the customer their finished goods.

The Value Chain for Software Engineering

Since the house project observation was so educational for Luke, I decided to try it again, but this time with software instead of houses. Luke had expressed an interest in helping me with the database design for the computing system I would build to assist him in his lemon business. I called some old IT friends and requested a few visits to show us a real IT software project in action. After eliminating the IT projects that looked too chaotic, we found a nice small project that was on track enough to spend some time with Luke. My friend Rachel offered to let us sit in on design sessions over the next three months to observe the process.

Ray's House Project	Rachel's Software Project
Scope	Scope
Owner's View	Owner's View
Architect's View	Logical Information System Designer's View
Builder's View	Physical Information System Designer's View

Ray's House Project	Rachel's Software Project
Subcontract's View	Developer's and Tester's View
Finished House	Finished System

LEVEL 1 – DEFINING THE SCOPE

Our first visit with Rachel's IT project was a review of the "return on investment" calculations for various scopes of resources, time, and features. This conversation reminded me of the Smith family, where the kids wanted a media room with all the features of Disneyland. The business wanted huge features with minimal time and resources to make their return on investment look earth-shaking. The IT staff held their ground, insisting that in the real world of IT the resources and time estimates should be an order of magnitude greater.

After an hour and a half of heated debate, everyone settled on a single scope statement that included a modest and realistic return on investment with reasonable amounts of resources, time, and features. The purpose of this Level 1 deliverable of scope is to assure that the timeframe, price, and features of the system meet the business owner's needs and budget.

LEVEL 2 – DESIGNING THE OWNER'S VIEW

For our next visit, Rachel referred us to Mike, who was the project's Conceptual Modeler. Mike walked us through the conceptual value chain model and the conceptual data model. They were both crystal clear as to what would happen in the business after the new system was delivered. Mike explained to Luke that conceptual data models are simple models that focus on the major aspects of the project that are of importance to the business owners who are sponsoring the project. All the details of how computers and software work are hidden in conceptual models since those details are not required for the business owner who is paying for the new system.

Luke crinkled his eyebrows and looked at the ceiling as he recalled the cardboard house that Ray produced for the family shopping for a new house. Yes, the conceptual model serves the same purpose as the cardboard house did in the house project. During the review, there were some IT people present and some business people who had been developers of software in a previous incarnation. Both groups tended to discuss server performance issues and network latency issues. Mike would gently reel them in by reminding them that these conceptual models are not a computing system design and therefore cannot have slow response times.

When the group returned to the topic of the conceptual models, they did uncover some missing pieces and a few things that were out of scope. The scope statement was ambiguous about these things. The conceptual models removed all the ambiguity from the short and simple scope statement from Level 1. The purpose of this Level 2 deliverable of the owner's view is to add enough details to the scope statement to ensure the business owner clearly and fully understands what he will be getting for his money and when he will be getting it.

LEVEL 3 – DESIGNING THE LOGICAL INFORMATION SYSTEM DESIGNER'S VIEW

Our next call from Rachel was to introduce us to James, the project's Logical Modeler. He was holding a design session with the IT architects and a few key developers. James was running into the same issues as Mike. The meeting contained several technology experts, and during the session, they kept discussing technologies, supportability, availability, and performance. Since the logical model is independent of all technology considerations, James would gently reel them in and return to the topic at hand, which was logical value chain and logical data modeling.

It was interesting to see how James would take the processes and entities from the conceptual models, elaborate on them to develop finely detailed processes and entities with attributes, and then abstract them into higher-level processes and entities. He showed us how these abstractions provide the flexibility to easily change the system as the business evolves.

Luke got lost at this phase. He understood the scope statement and the conceptual models, since they were at a low level of abstraction, but the logical models were beyond his young mind's ability to comprehend. Abstraction in design would need several additional learning sessions before Luke would understand. The purpose of this Level 3 deliverable of the logical model is to abstract the conceptual models into easily changeable structures and to partially communicate to the business owners about the system you will be building. But mostly, it is to communicate to the designers and builders of the physical system.

LEVEL 4 – DESIGNING THE PHYSICAL INFORMATION SYSTEM DESIGNER'S VIEW

Rachel sent an email to us to schedule the meeting with Louise, the project's Physical Modeler. Louise knew the database technology backwards and forwards. In our session, she took the logical models and structured them to match the technologies to be used in building the system. Focus on technology, supportability, availability, and performance was encouraged, since these physical models must leverage the strengths of the technologies while avoiding their weaknesses. The purpose of the Level 4 deliverable of the physical model is to enable building the data structures that will store data about the business in a specific database technology.

LEVEL 5 – BUILDING THE DEVELOPER'S AND TESTER'S VIEW

Rachel did not want Luke and me to bother the developers and testers as they did detail design and coding work, so we browsed the source code tree to view the code and test cases that were developed. Luke was totally bored with this exercise, but he did perk up when the database schema diagram was reviewed. The purpose of the Level 5 deliverable is to provide the software, installation instructions, and hardware requirements for those who will install the finished hardware and software solution.

LEVEL 6 – APPRECIATING THE FINISHED SYSTEM

Rachel let us visit the business site to watch the users of the new system as they took support calls from people who bought products and needed some help getting the full value from the products.

Luke was able to identify portions of the user interface that corresponded to pieces of the database schema diagram. That evening, after a wrestling and tickling match on the living room floor, Luke stopped for a moment, looked up at me, and said, "Dad, I want to learn how to data model." I tried not to look shocked and euphoric as I pseudo-calmly replied that we would start tomorrow. Just before bedtime, I introduced Luke to the Zachman Framework, developed by one of the many brilliant IBM research and development employees in the 1960s and 1970s. The Zachman Framework looks at how people design and build things.

He was pretty confused during my lecture—and sleepy—so I related the Zachman Framework to the house and software projects we had recently observed. Since all six levels of the Zachman Framework for engineering align well with the six levels of the house and software projects, Luke finally got it well enough that we could turn out the lights and tell stories until the sound of his sleeping breath signaled that dad was officially on break for this day.

House Project	Software Project	Zachman Framework
Scope	Scope	Contextual
Owner's View	Owner's View	Conceptual Data Model
Architect's View	Logical Information System Designer's View	Logical Data Model
Builder's View	Physical Information System Designer's View	Physical Data Model
Subcontractors' View	Code & Testing View	As Built
Finished House	Finished System	Functioning Deliverable

Key Points

- To deliver successful projects for houses, software, or any product or service, we need a balance of structure and creativity.

- The structure comes from following the engineering value chain, where we design the general deliverable before designing the specific deliverable.

- The creativity comes from delivering unique designs, using innovative building processes, and inventing methods for accurate, timely measurements of progress through the engineering value chain.

- And, all of these engineering processes are happening in feedback loops that trigger re-design, re-build, and re-measurement.

Models of the Real World

The next morning, we started with an introduction of what a model is as Luke's first data modeling lesson. *A model is a microcosm of some aspect of the real world.* Luke looked confused, so I clarified that a microcosm is a small pattern that matches a large pattern. For example, the real world contains some large patterns within the scope of a railroad. We built a model railroad that has the same patterns, but on a smaller scale. I remember that the model railroad in our basement was operated by Luke until the tracks were worn smooth. Our model railroad in the basement is a *microcosm of the real world* of trains. Good models can simulate most real world events with clear and common sense relationships between real world events and the corresponding model entities.

A data model represents the persons, places, things, events, or measurements required by a business (or any aspect of the real world). The data model contains the minimum set of relationship rules required to maintain consistency between the data model entities. Each entity has one or more uniqueness constraints so that we can differentiate one thing from another thing. Each entity also has a set of attributes that describe the entity. Data models are precise and cover lots of information in a single picture.

The combinatorial pathways (unique SQL statements) for navigating through a medium-sized model are in the millions. Correspondingly, the real world business event combinatorial pathways through a medium-sized business are in the millions as well. A good data model represents the set of information pathways that match the real world business execution pathways. The data model will contain both "currently used pathways" and "waiting to be used pathways." When the business asks for new pathways, they should already exist in the pool of "waiting to be used pathways." This means new business needs can be met without logical data model or physical database schema changes. Good data models are isomorphic (similar in structure and function) to the real world "scope" or "aspect" being modeled. Good data models also contain abstraction in the right places and at the right level based on the stage of the data engineering lifecycle (conceptual, logical, physical). Good models also accommodate the needs of the business for flexibility when business changes trigger computing system changes.

Luke was clearly daydreaming during our discussion, so we went to the basement and played with the model train set while I replayed some of the concepts. This seemed to help. It was refreshing to dust off the old train set and get it running again. It reminded me of the days when Luke's imagination turned our model railroad into a real steam engine thundering down the tracks. Watching children use their imaginations to turn inanimate toys into living adventures makes my adult analytical brain feel humbled and a bit bored. Luke was ready now to move on to the idea of tabular data storage since the idea of models was mostly clear to him.

Key Points

- Models are good ways to organize our thinking about the real world without having to interact with real world objects.

- Models are easy to analyze since time and space are compressed into a few diagrams and definitions.

- Models make explicit the interdependences of entity/entity, entity/process, and process/process.

- It is better to find problems in models than it is to build real world things and only then find problems with the things we paid to build.

- We can use models to:
    - Simulate real world events to remove inefficiencies and tune models.
    - Develop a single vocabulary and a value chain for all employees, and partners, and customers.
    - Serve as a baseline for computing system construction (IT).
    - Serve as a baseline for business processes execution instructions (people).

Chapter 4
Tabular Data Storage

Data models are built upon a method of storing data called tabular storage. We must understand this way of storing data to understand data models. Tabular data storage can also be called *relational* data storage. For examples, I showed Luke the bus schedule, phone book, and a spreadsheet I named **Person**. Tabular data storage in the physical data model consists of tables which contain columns and rows:

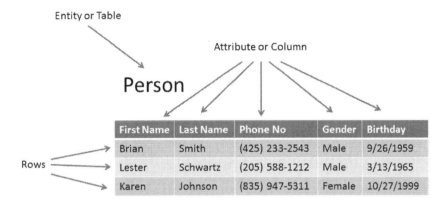

Tables and columns are referred to by different terms based on the type of data model being produced. While the idea is the same for all types of data models, the physical model uses the terms table and column. Conceptual, logical, and physical will be defined shortly. Here are the names and completeness required for each data model type:

Data Model Type	Container Name	Property Name	Property Completeness
Conceptual Data Model	Entity	Attribute	Main attributes needed to make clear to owner what he is buying. Need not be normalized. Can describe master data, transactional data, or measurement data.
Logical Data Model	Entity	Attribute	Entities contain all attributes needed by the system being designed. Needs to be fully normalized for master data and transactional data. Can describe measurement data.
Physical Data Model	Table	Column	All columns needed for the next phase of delivery for master data, transactional data, and measurement data.

Luke seemed to get the tabular idea and wanted to understand more about the conceptual versus the logical data model. This would require Luke to understand the notion of abstraction. I was worried that abstraction would be out of his grasp at age nine, but we gave it a try.

Abstraction

Luke jumped onto Wikipedia.org and looked up *abstraction*:

> **Abstraction** *is a process by which higher concepts are derived from the usage and classification of literal ("real" or "concrete") concepts. "An abstraction" is the product of this process: a concept that acts as a super-categorical noun for all subordinate concepts, and connects any related concepts as a group, field, or category.*

Of course, this definition left both of us more confused than we were originally. I tried a simpler approach. Things can be modeled specifically or they can be modeled with generality. When models are specific, they are clear, obvious, and easily understood. When models are generalized, they are unclear, hidden, and hard to understand.

Sounds like an easy decision between which abstraction style to choose, right? Wait, there is catch: specific models are more susceptible to data structure change while generalized models are less susceptible to data structure change.

On the other hand, generalized models may be more complex to process against because you always have to find the data you need—it's not explicitly laid out for you. The cost of change in computing systems is way too high in most businesses. I tried some simple examples. I had Luke create a general abstraction that covered all the things in my list of specifics. I started with obvious examples to solidify his confidence.

Specific things from dad	General abstraction from Luke
• Leather ball • Rubber ball • Plastic ball	• Ball

Yes Luke, this is correct. Now let's try a harder one:

Specific things from dad	General abstraction from Luke
• Reptile • Mammal • Bird • Fish	• Animal

Correct again. Now let's try a really hard one:

Specific things from dad	General abstraction from Luke
• Baseball • Basketball • Tennis ball	• Ball

This was mostly correct, but to lead him toward a new data model abstraction, I added one more thing to his abstraction of "Ball." I called it "Sport". Technically the first example of leather ball, rubber ball and plastic ball requires the abstraction of ball as well as the abstraction of material type. Now he understood that to abstract some sets of specific things, you may need two or more general things to fully cover the specific things:

Specific things from dad	General abstraction from Luke
• Principal • Teacher • Counselor • Nurse • Student • Janitor	• Person • School Job Type

This was an excellent answer and showed that Luke was grasping abstraction much better than I imagined for his first lesson. Next one:

Specific things from dad	General abstraction from Luke
• General • Major • Sergeant • Lieutenant • Private	• Solider • Rank

Another correct answer; Luke was on an abstraction roll!

Specific things from dad	General abstraction from Luke
• Tree • Trunk • Roots • Branch • Twig • Leaves	• Tree

This was wrong since the specific thing and the general thing cannot be the same, and "Tree" is in both. I was fishing for a recursive abstraction and had him try again. He said "Plant." Not a bad abstraction, but think about the "Rank" entity that helped "Soldier" to be a complete abstraction. Can you think of a helper generalization that can help "Plant" cover the large and small pieces of the tree? Luke came up with the entity "Chunk," and then immediately changed it to "Plant Part Type," Both answers solved the problem. Next one:

Specific things from dad	General abstraction from Luke
• Airplane • Body • Wing • Engine • Seats • Doors • Avionics • Hydraulics	• Airplane Part • Bill of Materials

Luke got this one right since his dad had spent 16 years working at Boeing Airplane Company and we had toured the factory several times. Now it was time to look at real data models and apply the principles from our abstraction game.

Key Points

- Models are abstractions of the real world things around us. Models themselves can be designed with various degrees of abstraction, from high to low.

- Low amounts of abstraction in a model yield a clear, obvious, and easily understood model. Business owners get value from these models since they can have a clear understanding of what it is they are buying. These models, unfortunately, require re-design and re-structuring when the business changes.

- High amounts of abstraction in a model yield a model that is hard to understand. Business owners do not get great value from these models. However, these models are easy to change when the business changes, so they are valuable for the computing system designers and builders.

Today's Project: Badminton

We had just spent an afternoon with our neighbors Anne and Julia, playing badminton until dark. It had been lots of fun, so I launched into this explanation of abstraction using badminton as the scope statement. The conceptual data model would be designed with specificity (low amount of abstraction) and the logical data model would be designed with generality (high amount of abstraction).

An entity is a person, place, thing, or event that exists within the scope of the project being modeled. What are the entities for our new software project called *badminton*?

CONCEPTUAL DATA MODEL

Conceptual data model entities should be designed with specificity and obvious clarity. Again, this is called a "low level of abstraction data design." This design approach is clear to business owners and does not require them to understand the data values that reside inside of entities. This approach is good for conceptual data models but is bad for logical and physical data models. When the rules of the business change, the CDM will often require data model redesign. It is acceptable to modify the structure of the CDM when new business requirements arise since we don't have thousands of lines of code needing to be changed when the CDM changes.

Changing the structure of the information system logical and physical data models is usually not acceptable since changes to the system data structures can trigger costly recoding and retesting of thousands of lines of code in the system. The symbols and notation below will be explained in detail later. Since CDM and LDM have design principles at the entity/relationship level, I will leave out most of the attributes for this exercise. The attribute design principles will be covered later in the book under normalization. The following page contains the badminton CDM.

The subject areas are the large boxes:

  Location: The place where matches are played and where teams practice.
  Event: The matches played between two teams.
  Party: The people involved in badminton and their roles.
  Equipment: The items managed by each team.

Here is a description of each relationship:
* Badminton is played in a stadium that hosts matches.
* Each stadium contains seating sections for observers and courts where the teams play.
* Each match is between two teams, one home team and one away team.
* The match has rules enforced by a referee.

- Each match provides entertainment to the observers, who pay to watch the game.
- Teams are financed by their sponsor.
- Teams are given direction by their coaches.
- Teams field a set of players to engage in matches.
- The coaches manage the birdies for each match.
- The players use their rackets for each match.

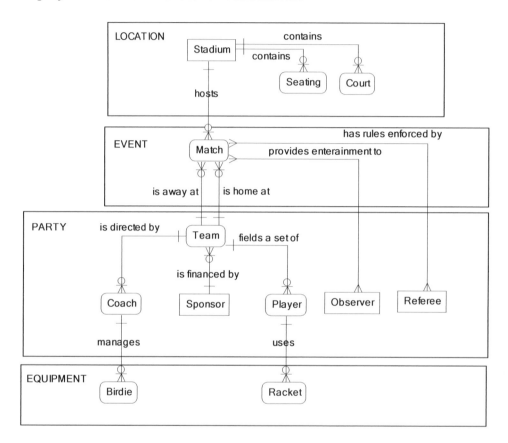

Here is a description of each entity:

- **Location**
    - **Stadium**–the place where matches are held
    - **Seating**–the place where spectators sit to watch the matches
    - **Court**–the place where the players engage in the match
- **Event**
    - **Match**–two badminton teams playing at a specific time and place
- **Party**
    - **Sponsor**–the organization that manages the finances
    - **Team**–the collection of players who compete in matches
    - **Coach**–the people who manage the team
    - **Player**–the athletes who play the matches

      o **Referee**–the person who enforces the rules

      o **Observer**–the people who purchase tickets and watch the matches

- **Equipment**
  - **Birdie**–the object that the players hit with the racket
  - **Racket**–the instrument that strikes the birdie

LOGICAL DATA MODEL

Logical data model entities should be designed with generality. This is called a "high level of abstraction data design." The LDM on the next page is a transformation of the CDM above. We have transformed the low-abstraction CDM to become a high-abstraction LDM.

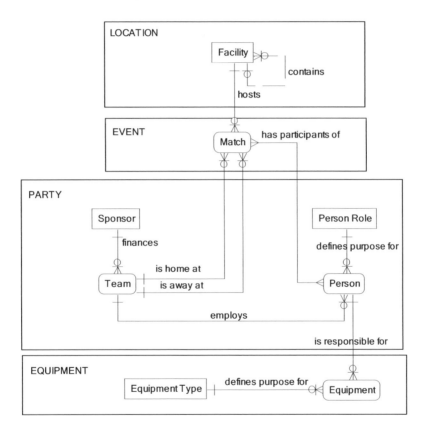

Here is a description of each relationship:

- A facility contains internal structures (seating, courts), which may themselves contain smaller internal structures.
- The facility is the host for each match.
- At a match there is one home team and one away team that will compete.
- A sponsor manages the finances for the team by collecting ticket revenue and paying the team's expenses.
- Each person has a purpose in a match.

- The team employs a group of people.
- Each person has equipment that they must manage.
- Equipment types define the purpose for each piece of equipment.

Here is a description of each entity:
- **Location**
  - **Facility**–the building and the internal structures used for matches. Internal structures may contain smaller structures
- **Event**
  - **Match**–the event where two teams compete
- **Party**
  - **Sponsor**–the organization that manages the finances
  - **Team**–the collection of players who compete in matches
  - **Person**–an individual who participates on the team
  - **Person Role**–the purpose for a person who participates on the team
- **Equipment**
  - **Equipment**–the things used by the team to engage in matches
  - **Equipment Type**–the function of each piece of equipment

This LDM design requires an understanding of the rows of data within some key master data entities such as **Equipment Type**. The only way to know that we are tracking *birdies* and *rackets* is to look inside of the **Equipment Type** entity to see the values. This approach is good for logical and physical data models since it is less susceptible to costly computing change when the rules of the business change.

The technique used to transform the Badminton CDM into the Badminton LDM is abstraction, as we are merging diverse and specific entities from the CDM into a smaller set of less diverse and more generalized entities in the LDM that can handle business changes without altering the data structure.

Subject Area	Specific Entities from CDM	General Entities from LDM
Party	Coach	Person
	Player	Person Role
	Referee	
	Observer	
Equipment	Birdie	Equipment
	Racket	Equipment Type
Location	Stadium	Facility
	Seating	Sub-Facility
	Court	Sub-Facility

The sample data values in the diagram below show the main rows of master data needed to understand the meaning of the LDM.

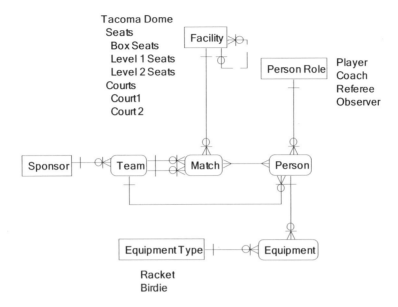

The facility entity has a relationship to itself. This means that a facility may have sub-facilities.

Parent Facility	Sub-Facility
Tacoma Dome	Seats
Tacoma Dome	Courts
Seats	Box Seats
Seats	Level 1 Seats
Seats	Level 2 Seats
Courts	Court 1
Courts	Court 2

Data Model Evolution

After a long silence, Luke asked what happens when we need to change things due to people changing their minds about how to run a badminton team. Well, let us imagine that a change happens in our aspect of the world called "badminton."

The boss announces that next quarter all teams will have trainers to manage medical issues with the players. He had recently been sued by a player who had hurt his leg but continued to play and now is permanently in pain. The cost of the trainer will be nothing compared to the cost of losing a law suit. The trainers will have medical supplies that are used to treat the players for problems they experience in the games. Our CDM (low abstraction) design will have to change schema structure (this is okay) by adding two entities **Trainer** and **Medical Supply**. On the facing page the top model is the badminton conceptual data model after making this change.

The LDM is a general (high abstraction) data model, so it will remain stable across the boss' new change. We will merely need to add rows to the database represented by the LDM. This is a quick, easy, and cheap way to change the data model and the database. Add a row of data to **Person Role** for `Trainer` and add a row of data to **Equipment Type** for `Medical Supply`.

Now the LDM and the related physical data model are ready to start recording new trainer and medical supply information. Here is the badminton logical data model after making this change.

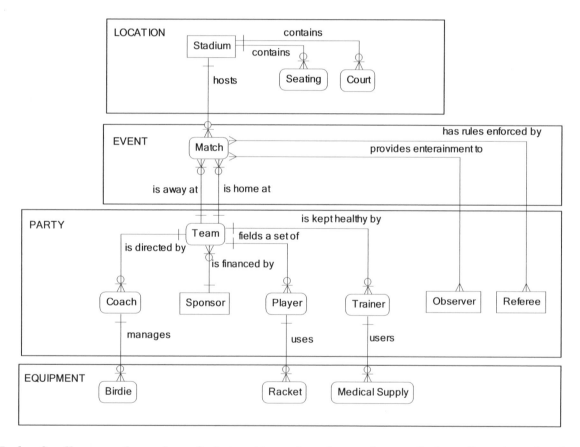

Luke finally saw the value of abstraction when he understood that changing the data structure would impact lots of code and be costly to implement, while changing the rows of data was fast, cheap, and easy. Later, we will discuss how over-abstraction in the logical model can lead to confusion and problems.

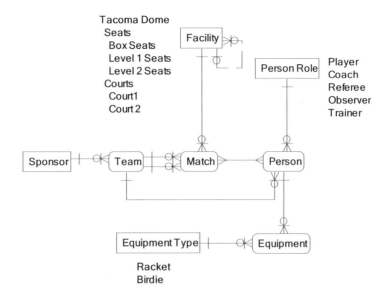

Then, quite to my surprise, Luke got a perplexed look on his face and asked how my abstracted logical data model handles the fact that birdies have a feather count and rackets have a string tension? Luke observed that the CDM had separate entities for **Birdie** and **Racket** and that each of these entities had their own separate attributes. He asked where these attributes belong in the LDM, and how we keep people from recording string tension on a birdie and keep people from recording feather count on a racket.

I was floored and had to reevaluate Luke's ability to listen, understand, and analyze. He had just turned 10 years old the week before, but I never expected this response. Sometimes I forget that children have more functional neurons in their brains than we adults. Getting those neurons to infer sophisticated paradoxes from an LDM is rare, so I attributed this epiphany to his intelligence and my teaching ability. Now I was in recovery mode and had to scramble to avoid embarrassment. First, I explained an entity called **Attribute** and described how this is used to handle the attributes that are specific to different types of equipment. The entity **Attribute** is a red flag for potential over-abstraction. Next, I pointed out that there are attributes that all types of equipment have in common, such as:

- Equipment Id
- Asset Tag Number
- Equipment Name
- Purchase Date
- Purchase Price
- Condition Category

These attributes are characteristics of the entity **Equipment** and belong in that entity. Now some attributes apply specifically to certain types of equipment, like the birdie attribute of feather count and the racket attribute of string tension. In this case, we need an entity to allow our information system to maintain a rapid and cost-effective capability to change as business needs change and to ensure that each type of **Equipment** has the proper set of attributes. I quickly got into my data modeling tool and pounded out a model to illustrate this design principle. See the model below.

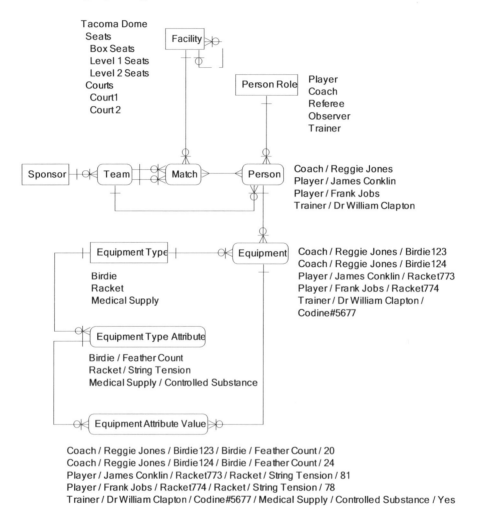

I added entities for **Equipment Type Attribute** to store the attributes unique to each **Equipment Type** and added **Equipment Attribute Value** to store the actual data contents for each **Equipment Type Attribute**. That is, the **Equipment Type Attribute** entity provides a list of the attributes that are valid for each type of equipment, while the **Equipment Attribute Value** entity contains the actual values for each person's piece of equipment.

Luke looked at it for a few minutes and agreed that this solved the problem he was thinking about, and he thanked me. I breathed a sigh of relief to know that my barely 10-year-old son had not out-data-modeled his 62-year-old dad.

Key Points

- Conceptual models are oriented to business owners and should be easily consumed by a broad group of business participants.

- Concepts are grouped into subject areas (large box around entities), and require structural redesign when business rules change.

- Logical models are oriented to information technology professionals, and should be structurally stable across business changes.

- Some selected group of business participants should understand the logical models. These business participants should not control content unless the logical model fails to fully support the conceptual model.

Over-Abstraction

Abstraction can be overdone, resulting in confusion in the logical model and poor system performance in the physical model. Abstraction can also be underdone, as we have noted previously, resulting in costly and time consuming changes to system code. Luke was dismayed to find out that abstraction, his recently acquired idea for doing good things, could be a bad thing when used in the extreme. I started out with a clearly ridiculous example of over-abstraction to entertain Luke:

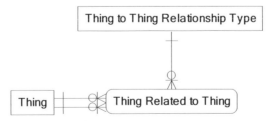

If this is our logical data model, we will have a problem being clear about when we are talking about *persons* and *roles* versus when we are talking about *medical equipment* and *medical equipment types*. This over-abstraction makes the normal amount of confusion on IT projects become an epidemic of severe confusion and rampant miscommunication. If this is our physical data model, we will have a problem with referential integrity and performance optimization.

If we have three tables in our database that match the diagram above, when the **Thing** called *customer* gets related to the **Thing** called *order*, the referential integrity between them and the transactional unit of work that records them must be coded by the developer. Further, the optimization of how to efficiently access customer and order data must be coded by the developer, and recoded when indexes change.

Physical Data Models

Luke asked about physical models, and since I would be the physical data modeler for the computing system running his lemon business, I felt obliged to respond briefly. If the CDM and LDM are done properly, the PDM, or physical data model, is relatively easy. The PDM design criteria vary from database product to database product since each product has different strengths and weaknesses. You must have a physical database designer who knows the technical strengths and weaknesses of the database product used to implement the PDM. Single server database systems, which execute instructions sequentially on one machine, are very different from the massively parallel processing database systems that are used for big data. Database systems that can only scale up (buy a larger server to get more performance) are very different from database systems that can scale out (add more servers to get more performance).

When I consider that Luke may well have another 90 years to interact with various database technologies, I can't imagine the capacity and features that he will have when he is an old man like his dad is today. I imagine Luke as a retired curmudgeon who queries big data using brainwaves and gets the answers injected directly into his brain. I also imagine him defining the semantics of data with the same CDM and LDM principles that he is learning today.

Key Points

- Physical database technology will change every day, and over a period of years will become unrecognizable to guys like yours truly, "dinosaur dad" (Luke's moniker for me).

- But the mental process for designing information systems has been stable for over 50 years now, so learning CDM, LDM, and value chain should be valuable for another 50 years or so.

- Abstraction can be a good thing, but it can also be a bad thing. Especially in the PDM, over-abstraction can cost more than it saves.

Chapter 5
Data Model Components

The next day I started in with Luke to define some of the major components of data models. The first major topic for Luke was *uniqueness*.

I had the opportunity to work briefly with Ted Codd at IBM in the late 1970s. I thought it would be good to get in some name dropping to increase my "cool factor" with Luke. Unfortunately he had never heard of Ted and therefore was unimpressed with my brief but educational encounter with the founder of my discipline. Ted Codd, the inventor of relational data modeling and the SQL programming language, said that uniqueness was one of the most important issues in data modeling. He said that we can understand and evaluate the real world because our brains can distinguish *one thing* from *another thing*.

For example, people are built by their DNA to have unique facial characteristics, and our eyes and brains are built by our DNA to recognize each person uniquely. This allows us to know specifically who is helping us and who is not helping us and then reciprocate appropriately. In our caveman days, reciprocation for not helping was usually implemented with a club to the head. Today, we tend to see more dialog, compromise, forgiveness, and collaboration. Well, uh, at times...

If our computing systems are going to understand and evaluate, they must have the same ability to distinguish *one thing* from *another thing*.

Uniqueness Constraints

Uniqueness constraints are how we distinguish *one thing* from *another thing* in a data model and in a physical database. I asked Luke to pick an entity and tell me what attributes are required to uniquely identify instances of that entity. He picked the entity **Person**, a particularly slippery species when it comes to unique identification in data models. I got Luke to go to the whiteboard and list the attributes necessary to uniquely identify persons.

He started with the typical suspects like:

- First Name
- Last Name
- Address
- Phone Number

I, of course, pointed out that two `Bill Smiths` can live in the same apartment and share a single landline for phone calls. In that case, the data model can store the first `Bill Smith`, but when his roommate `Bill Smith` comes along, the uniqueness constraint will stop him from entering the system. Stumped for the moment, Luke renewed his attack. He tried Social Security number (SSN). I asked for his Social Security number, and he admitted that he does not have one. This realization triggered a related thought that when he has his own business, legally I owe him his own SSN.

Now that both uniqueness attempts failed, he regrouped for another try. How about biometric measures of people like facial geometry, retina shape, fingerprint, or DNA? Yes, in certain business contexts, these are great attributes for uniqueness of **Person**. Luke asked for me to elaborate on "business contexts," and, being verbose, I gladly obliged.

To uniquely identify a Person, the context could be the level of security needed. High-security person identification needs, such as for handling nuclear waste disposal, may require biometric measures such as fingerprint, retina pattern, facial geometry, and DNA. Medium-security person identification needs, such as for purchasing software on the web, may require identity authentication such as through a Facebook account, Windows Live email account, etc. Low-security person identification needs, such as a Boy Scout recruiting sign up on a paper form at school event, may require user-supplied attributes such as first name, last name, address, phone number, and birth date.

Luke was able to see that depending on what you were trying to do, the information required could be very different. Unique keys can have different owners. Some keys are created by the business, and some keys are created by the computing system. Business keys are typically text or date data types. System keys are typically numeric.

When the data modeler has multiple unique keys on a single entity, she must choose one and only one key as the primary key; all other unique keys become alternate keys. Below is a uniqueness example for the entity **Taxpayer**.

TaxpayerId	SocialSecurityNumber	FirstName	LastName	Number of Dependents
2245	606-513-1212	Shane	Patton	6
2246	606-513-1213	Frank	Nimmo	4
2247	606-513-1214	Karen	Johnson	2

A system key is a field containing a number that is generated by the system. In order to maintain uniqueness, no two rows in the same entity will ever have the same number. It is frequently a running sequence number that just keeps getting bigger as more rows are added. The TaxpayerId in the above example is a system key.

A natural key is an attribute of the entity that happens to be unique across all rows. For example, Social Security Number is unique to each individual, so if it were legal to do so, it could be used as a unique identifier for a **Person** (given system scope of US citizens).

It is often preferable to have a system key that is used internally by the system while also having a business key that is visible to and used by business users. When a natural key exists, it makes sense to use it as the business key. So the system would use TaxpayerId behind the scenes, while the business user of the system would see SocialSecurityNumber. Now one of those attributes must be picked as the primary key and the other must become the alternate key.

A primary key is the identifier that will be used to identify each unique record in an entity/table. An alternate key is an attribute/column in the same entity/table that could also be used to uniquely identify the record. All of the attributes/columns that could uniquely identify a record are called candidate keys. One is chosen to be the primary key and the others are alternate keys

The LDM should use the natural key as the primary key when only one exists. Where multiple natural keys exist, select the one that is the most stable (least likely to be updated). For this LDM, the primary key would be the Social Security number, and the Taxpayer Id would be the alternate key or left out completely. In the physical data model, the Taxpayer Id will be the primary key, and the Social Security number will become an alternate key. This is done so that if the natural key is changed, it will be changed in one and only one entity or table. Business users cannot change the Taxpayer Id since it is maintained behind the scenes and they are not aware of its existence.

Key Points

- Being able to discriminate one thing from another thing is a critical capability for both humans and computing systems to be successful.

- Uniqueness in the system that mirrors uniqueness in the real world is mandatory for computing system success.

- Things are unique while at the same time they are interdependent due to entity to entity relationships.

Relationships

Relationships are built in a data model by copying the primary key of an entity to become a foreign key in a neighboring entity. Each entity has a primary key that identifies unique instances within the entity. For example, Social Security number could be the primary key to entity **Taxpayer**. The neighbor entity called **Taxpayer Filing** is the history of a given taxpayer submitting his tax statement. The Social Security number in the **Taxpayer Filing** entity is called a foreign key.

Relationships are the silken strands that create a web of entities. This structure represents the pathways for traversing the data that are available to the consumers of the data.

Luke stopped me. His scrunched up forehead had confusion written on it, so I backed up and gave some examples. I went to my car and pulled out the auto club map of Florida. I asked Luke a silly question, "When we go from Jacksonville to Gainesville, how do we do it?" He replied that we travel on highway 412 East for about an hour. "OK. If we consider each city to be an entity and each highway to be a relationship, then this map of Florida is built like a data model is built. We traverse from city to city using the roads, and we traverse from entity to entity using the relationships."

Luke pulled out his cell phone and turned on his driving directions app. This app uses the Global Positioning System and a database of cities and highways. He asked if this driving directions database was an example of my example. Yes, he was correct. The driving directions app traverses the relationships in the database to find the optimal pathway for us to travel. Then we physically traverse the roads under the surveillance of GPS. Once again I was stunned to see him understanding my lesson to the point of applying it to the next layer of utility on his cell phone app. Luke sat in silence for a moment and then announced that he was ready to start his Relationship lecture. So I continued.

Each relationship has a purpose. Relationships are named with verb phrases to describe the nature of the relationship between the two entities being related. For example, Entity1 (verb) Entity2, so in the following diagram, Customer (places) Order, Child (owns) Toy, and Shipment (triggers) Invoice:

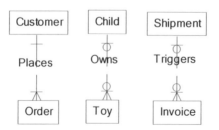

Referential integrity rules define how a collection of entities or tables are tied together to create a structure that can be traversed along the relationship pathways. Creating a relationship between two entities means that the primary key (PK) attributes of the entity where the relationship starts (parent entity) will be added to the entity where the relationship ends (child entity). These attributes are called a foreign key (FK) because they are not native to the entity and appear in the child entity because they have migrated via the relationship from the parent entity.

IDENTIFYING VS. NON-IDENTIFYING RELATIONSHIPS

In identifying relationships, the parent entity PK migrates to the child entity and becomes part of its PK. To identify unique instances of the **Room** child entity, I must know the **Building** parent entity that houses the room.

Non-identifying relationships have the parent entity PK migrating to the child entity, but not as part of the child PK. To identify unique instances of **Computer Equipment**, I do not need to know the Building Id and Room Number where it happens to be sitting at the moment.

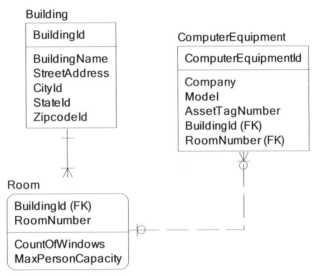

Attributes above the line are PK attributes. Building has an identifying relationship to Room (solid line). Room has a non-identifying relationship to Computer Equipment (dashed line).

- A **Building** can have one or more **Rooms**, so zero **Rooms** is not a possibility for a **Building**. A **Room** must be in a **Building**.
- A **Room** can have zero, one, or more **Computer Equipment**. A **Room** can be identified independent of the **Computer Equipment** in the **Room** at any moment. **Computer Equipment** can have one or zero **Rooms**. **Computer Equipment** can be identified independent of the **Room** where it sits at any moment.

Not Null FK means the relationship is mandatory, and all children must have the parent. Nullable FK means that a child can exist and not have the parent. In the example above,

Computer Equipment (child) may or may not have a **Room** (parent), so BuildingId and RoomId can be null attributes in the **Computer Equipment** entity.

Relationships are specified by this list of set intersection conditions:

- Zero, one, or more
- Zero or one
- One or more
- Exactly x

In the example of identifying relationships on the previous page, each **Building** has a Building Id, each **Room** has a Room Number, and every **Building** must have at least one **Room**. A **Building** with no **Rooms** is not a **Building** that my business cares to record, so there will be no rows in the **Room** entity with a null Building Id. This is due to the primary key rule that no part of a primary key can be missing or null. This means that when I insert a new **Room** row, the Building Id must be present. For you and me to meet at the right place for lunch today, I need to tell you both the Room Number and the Building Name. If I just say meet in `Room 1233`, then you may well go to the wrong building to meet me. I must say meet me in the `Smith Towers` Building in `Room 1233` for lunch today. The three identifying relationship types are below, starting left to right:

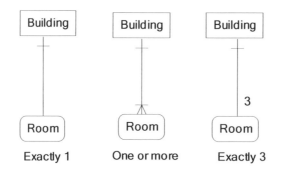

1. A **Building** must have one **Room**. A **Room** must always have one and only one **Building**.
2. A **Building** must have at least one **Room** and can have many **Rooms**. A **Room** must have one and only one **Building**.
3. A **Building** must have three **Rooms**. A **Room** must have one and only one **Building**.

I don't know of any businesses that actually have rules to limit their buildings to one or three rooms. The data model below shows identifying relationships that happen far more frequently. Read data model from left to right:

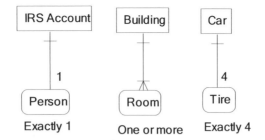

1. An **IRS Account** must have one **Person**. A **Person** must have one and only one **IRS Account**.
2. A **Building** must have a least one **Room** and may have many **Rooms**. A **Room** must have one and only one **Building**.
3. A **Car** must have four **Tires**. A **Tire** must be on one and only one **Car**.

In non-identifying relationships, attributes of a foreign key may be null. This was not true for the identifying examples above, where a null foreign key value was disallowed. In the examples below, every **Toy** may or may not belong to a **Child**. Also, I can identify a **Child** without any knowledge of **Toys**. Conversely I can identify **Toys** without any knowledge of the **Child** that owns the **Toy**.

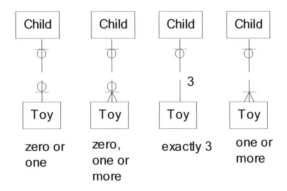

Of course Luke disliked most of these non-identifying relationship types. This is Luke's list of most hated relationship types reading from left to right:

1. *Zero or one* Toys for each Child (hates it; at most one toy can exist, and zero toys is possible)
2. *Zero, one, or more* Toys for each Child (dislikes zero as still being possible, one is lame, and more is the only hopeful sign)
3. *Exactly three* Toys for each Child (feels uneasy with just three, but is glad that zero, one, or two toys is impossible)
4. *One or more* Toys for each Child (happy that zero is impossible and more than three is possible)

ONE-TO-MANY RELATIONSHIPS

Luke wanted to data model people and baseball tickets since we recently attended a pre-season professional game. So we did a data model of **Person** and **Baseball Ticket**. Luke insisted on specifying the referential integrity rules for the relationship between a person and a baseball ticket. Here is the model and a description of each rule appears below the model:

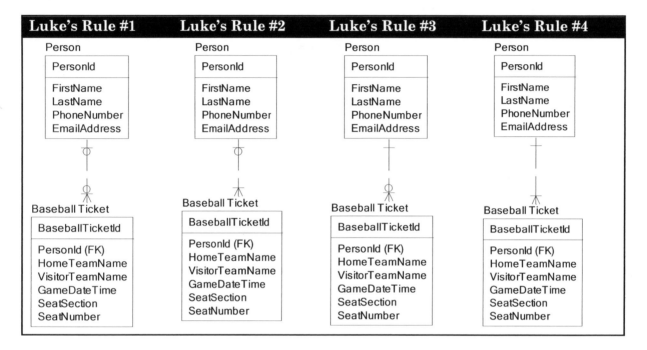

- Luke's Rule #1: A **Person** may have no **Tickets** and a **Ticket** may have no **Person** in the model below. This is indicated by the circle near baseball ticket, meaning a person may have no ticket. The circle near the person means that a ticket can have no person.
- Luke's Rule #2: Then Luke said that he wants every **Person** to always have a **Ticket**, so I removed the O from the baseball ticket side of the relationship and added a bar, meaning the person must have at least one ticket to be created in this data model.
- Luke's Rule #3: Then Luke said, "No, I meant to say that I want every ticket to always belong to a person, and a person can exist with no tickets."
- Luke's Rule #4: Then, just to aggravate me, he said, "No, I meant to say that every ticket has to belong to a person, and every person has to have a ticket," so I calmly changed the model again.

MANY-TO-MANY RELATIONSHIPS

I let Luke pick the topic of this modeling section. He selected his hobbies and friends as the scope statement for our many-to-many data modeling lesson. I asked the following questions of Luke: "For a given Friend, say Cyrus, how many hobbies can you play with him?" He responded that Cyrus plays basketball and badminton. "For a given Hobby, say basketball, how many friends play this hobby?" He responded, "I play basketball with Cyrus, Aden, and Tristan."

Luke got up to the whiteboard and fished around to data model this project using two entities. No matter how he tried, it failed. I suggested he try modeling this problem with three entities and voila, it worked. His finished data model is below:

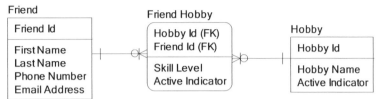

The entity in the middle is called either a many-to-many associative entity or an intersection entity; the terms are synonymous. I asked Luke to explain his data model, so he stated: A friend may stop doing a hobby that I am still doing, so the Active Indicator in the entity **Friend Hobby** tells us if a friend is still engaging in the hobby. An inactive friend for a hobby may suddenly become active, so we'd flip his Active Indicator back on. Further, I may choose to stop participating in some hobby for some period of time, so I can set the Active Indicator in the **Hobby** entity to falsely to show that I no longer do this hobby. If I chose to restart the **Hobby**, I still have a record of all my **Friends** who formerly played the hobby with me.

I requested that we put an Active Indicator in the **Friend** entity, so he can un-friend his friends. Then I suggested we just delete the row for that **Friend** when he wants to un-friend a former **Friend**. Luke properly pointed out that a physical delete would not allow him to easily change his mind and re-friend his formerly un-friended friend while retaining all the information about that friend and his hobbies. So I agreed, and we added the Active Indicator attribute to the **Friend** entity. As a general rule, the Active Indicator attribute applies to most entities.

RECURSIVE RELATIONSHIPS

Recursive relationships are another topic I was worried that Luke might not be ready to understand. Recursive relationships exist when the rows of an entity relate to other rows in the same entity. For example, some **Product** rows are related to other **Product** rows. I told Luke the real-life story of my first recursive encounter:

As a boy of about four years old, I awoke late one Saturday morning to the call of breakfast on the table. I sat down half asleep and grabbed a box of cereal. I looked at the front of the box hoping to find my favorite sugar-laden brand, but found a new healthy cereal instead. On the front of the box was a picture of a baseball player holding a box of the cereal, and, of course, on the small box he was holding was an even smaller baseball player holding an even smaller box, etc. Well, I had the strangest sense of tumbling head over heels, as I felt like I was falling in slow motion into the picture on the front of the box. I closed my eyes to make the sensation stop, but I continued falling into the black hole of recursion. My mom saw my troubled look and asked if I was okay. I opened my eyes and was glad to see that I was still outside of the box, firmly anchored into my chair. I was relieved to still be full size and was glad to have stopped tumbling into the picture. I was fully awake by now, felt a bit shaky, and had lost my appetite.

Luke asked me if I had seen *Alice in Wonderland* when she fell down the rabbit hole. Come to think of it, I had seen that movie at about the time. I warned Luke to never take his children go see *Alice in Wonderland* followed by exposure to recursion. Luke replied that he would have no children since fifth grade girls were so yucky that marriage was too disgusting to consider possible. I suggested that his views will change with his hormones, but he rejected my prediction. Luke shook his finger at me saying, "Dad, you are old fashioned. You don't understand fifth grade girls these days."

Meanwhile, old-fashioned Dad and new-fashioned Luke were not progressing on his recursion lesson, so I continued. Recursive relationships exist in two types:

1. One-to-Many Recursive Relationships
2. Many-to-Many Recursive Relationships

First, for one-to-many recursive relationships, the classic example is the military hierarchy:

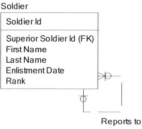

Each soldier row has one and only one row in the **Soldier** entity. Each also has one and only one value in the attribute Superior Soldier Id. This means that each soldier reports to one and only one superior. Each superior can have many subordinate soldiers, since the foreign key attribute of Superior Soldier Id is not unique in the entity. If I am a General and my Soldier Id is 344, and if I have three subordinates, then the attribute Superior Soldier Id will have three rows with the value 344 for my three subordinates Frank, Bruce, and John:

Soldier Id	First Name	Last Name	Superior Soldier Id	Rank
344	Brian	Shive	null	General
345	Frank	Lee	344	Colonel
346	Bruce	Jamison	344	Colonel
347	John	Johnson	344	Colonel

The top soldier has a null value for his row in the attribute Superior Soldier Id. This top soldier may report to the President, who is a civilian and is not in the Soldier entity.

Luke requested that we data model the topic of families using one-to-many recursion, but we could not do this since each child has many parents, and the rule for one-to-many recursion is that each subordinate has one superior. So one-to-many recursion cannot model families, but Luke's suggestion indicated his brain was tracking the concept of recursion.

This led us to many-to-many recursive relationships. In many-to-many recursion, we need to introduce the ideas that one child can have many parents and one parent can have many children. Data modeling a simple thing like a family is surprisingly difficult, with dozens of valid design options and no clear winner for all business contexts. Other seemingly complex things like manufacturing can be surprisingly easy to data model with clear winners and losers. Below is one data model for Family. The entity **Family Structure** is a many-to-many recursive associative entity.

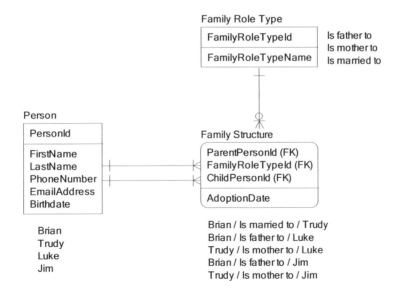

The model above allows for polygamy (one man has many wives). To avoid breaking the law, the data model can use one-to-one recursion for marriage to disallow polygamy, as shown below:

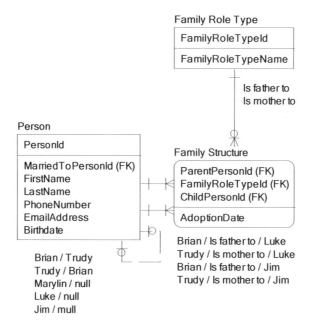

Now each Person row can have one and only one Married To Person Id value, so we conform to the polygamy laws. Also, each child can have many parents and each parent can have many children.

There are two unique constraints on the **Person** entity above:

- Person Id attribute is unique
- Married To Person Id is unique, when present

This is how we get one husband and one wife enforced using one-to-one recursion. For single people, the Married to Person Id is null. Luke was lost in the clouds that often obscure the topic of recursion, so I thought it best to wrap up the topic and bike to the park.

We would return to attempt to scale the Mount Everest of recursion by climbing the concept of many-to-many recursive relationships. There exists a process called many-to-many recursion explosion. This process starts with an entry point and finds related rows that are chained to the entry point. For example, an explosion of the **Person** and **Family** entities could start with **Person** = `Brian Shive` as the seed condition, and then traverse neighboring links to find all rows related to `Brian Shive`. The explosion traversal rules could include:

- Just my children
- Just my parents
- Both my children and my parents

- Just my grandparents
- Both my grandparents and my parents
- Both my grandparents and my children

...lots of traversal routes possible...You can fall into the rabbit hole following many pathways.

Luke demanded a break from the lecture, so we went out on the deck and had some hot chocolate and toast. I told Luke that we would resume shortly and he could pick the topic for our final recursion lesson. Luke had recently enjoyed disassembling our broken toaster. He asked for a recursion lesson on toasters, so we returned to our lesson with toasters in our sights.

The classic example of directed graph traversal is **Bill of Materials** for **Products**. If I design my products using **Part Numbers** in a many-to-many recursive structure, I can easily find the total quantity of **Part Numbers** that need to be ordered to support my factory. In the example below, I am designing and manufacturing toasters.

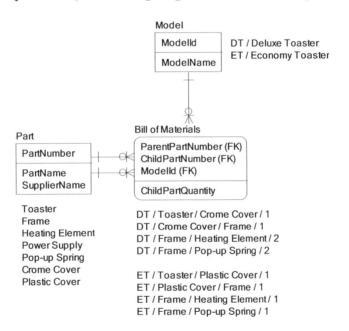

I have two models of toasters, the `Deluxe Toaster` and the `Economy Toaster`. I am forecasting next month's needs for parts, given a forecast of next month's sales. My sales staff assures me they will move 800 deluxe units and 1200 cheap units. I must determine how many parts we will need next month.

We first need to enter the **Bill of Materials** in the **Model** table using seed quantities of 800 Deluxe Toasters and 1200 Economy Toasters. Then we can explode from the parent parts to the child parts, and add up the child quantities along the traversal chain to determine the order quantity for each part for next month until there are no more child parts found for all pathways. Next we determine the delta between "parts on hand" and "next month's parts requirements", and order additional parts to fill the parts on hand deficit.

The From –> To pairs of linked nodes create networks of pathways to traverse. These pathways can have different patterns. There are both directed acyclic and directed cyclic graphs. Directed acyclic graphs contain node pairs that have a direction and always find an edge when traversing from the entry point node to all neighbors, examples include:

- Parent Animal –> Offspring Animal
- Assembly Part –> Component Part
- Component Part –> Raw Material

Directed acyclic graphs contain node pairs that have a direction and may never find an edge node due to an infinite loop of links, examples include:

- From Network Router Node -> To Network Router Node
- Friend -> Friended Friend

Luke had been curiously silent and motionless. For a talkative squirmy boy, this worried me. I asked him to summarize today's lesson on recursion. He blurted out his frustrations and confusion, asking for me to "pleeease do the summary." I stood my ground and insisted that Luke try a brief summary. Squirming and anxious, Luke said "I'd like to curse once now, and then I will re-curse again later. No, seriously dad, I am lost on this topic." I granted a reprieve and summarized recursion on his behalf.

Key Points

- Recursive data models are good at describing the fact that product and service designs exist at different scales, such as starting with a "big" thing like a toaster and ending with a small component such as a spring release:
  - Deluxe Toaster → Frame → Heating Element → Spring Release

- When we build a product or service from its design, we construct big finished goods from small components.

Luke and I covered one last lesson on relationship design.

OCCAM'S RAZOR FOR RELATIONSHIP DESIGN

William of Occam said that when two theories are competing on a single topic, the theory with the fewest assumptions wins. While designing relationships in a data model, the model with no redundant relationships wins. Luke jumped in and requested we use a school as the example for redundant relationships that violate Occam's rule of simplicity.

I obliged by developing the diagram on the next page, where all of the relationship lines that are dashed are redundant and should be removed. The four redundant relationships are labeled A, B, C, and D:

A. Course Offering already has the Building Id since it came from the Room to Course Offering relationship (solid line).

B. Course Offering already has Teacher Id since it came from the Certification to Course Offering relationship (solid line).

C. Course Offering already has the Course Type Id since it came from the Certification to Course Offering relationship (solid line).

D. Enrollment already has the Course Offering Time Period Id since it came from the Course Offering to Enrollment relationship (solid line).

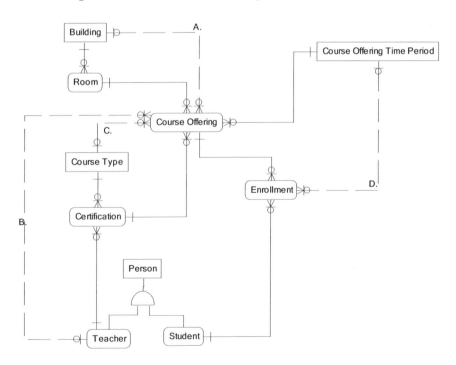

The data model on the next page is the proper model with no redundant relationships:

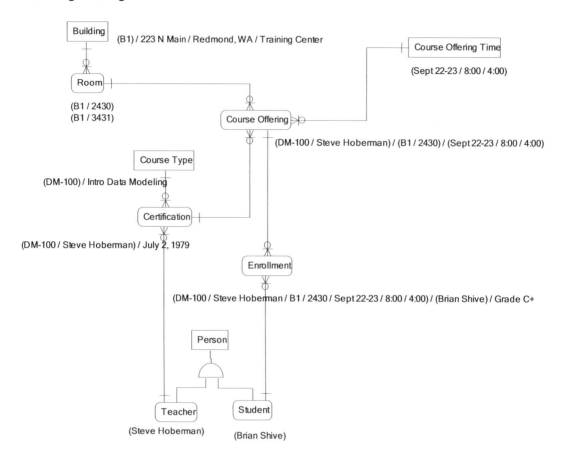

CLASSIFICATION HIERARCHIES

Classification hierarchies have two types of participant entities, the super-type entity and the sub-type entities under the super-type. The super-type entity is an abstraction that covers all the sub-type entities. Abstraction provides simplification of the data model and stability when the business changes requirements. The super-type entity contains the attributes that all sub-type entities have in common. The sub-type entities have attributes that are unique to themselves.

Exclusive vs. Inclusive Sub-types

In exclusive sub-types, each member of the super-type can be present in only one of the sub-types. In the following example, each child is either a male or a female. No person is both. The "x" in the symbol means exclusive sub-types. With inclusive sub-types, each member of the super-type can be one or more of the sub-types. In the following example, a person can be both a teacher for some classes and can be a student for other classes. Teachers can enroll as students. The absence of an "x" in the symbol means inclusive sub-types.

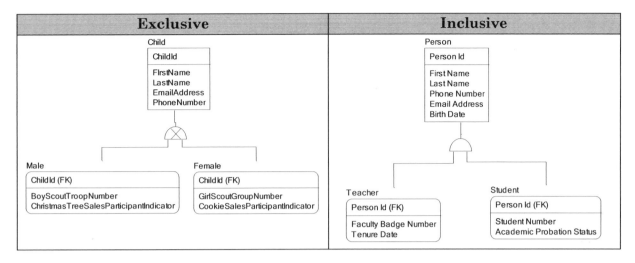

Complete vs. Incomplete Sub-types

In complete sub-types, the set of sub-types shown is the full set expected to be tracked by the business. For example, the **Male** and **Female** sub-types could be the complete set of sub-types expected to be used by a business. The complete indicator in this notation is the double lines under the circle. With incomplete sub-types, the set of sub-types is expected to be extended as the business evolves over time. For example, a school may data model just teachers and students, knowing that later there will be janitors, counselors, and other types of person tracked in their school. The single line under the sub-type symbol in this notation indicates an incomplete sub-type.

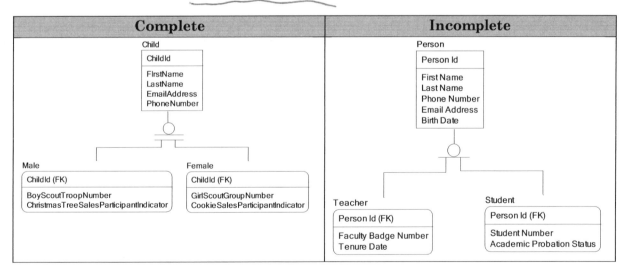

On the next page is a classification hierarchy for the entity **Animal**:

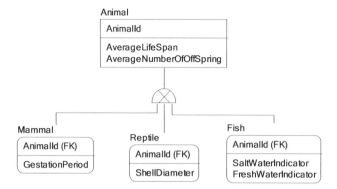

Since Luke and I had a fun visit with the house building project, I tried an example of construction parts:

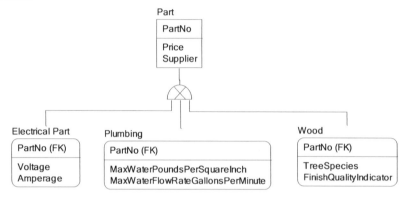

Luke wondered about the value of classification hierarchy. I explained that it is like his example of the badminton birdie having a Feather Count attribute and the racket having a String Tension attribute:

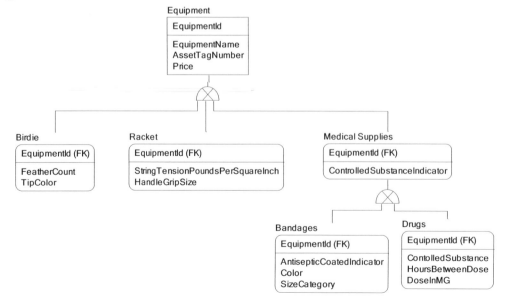

In classification hierarchies, we can specify at the CDM level which attributes belong to which entities, as we have done in the Part classification hierarchy above. Then, in the LDM and PDM, we can abstract the attributes to make them easily extensible when the business demands change. This involves an entity called **Attribute** and must be done carefully to avoid over abstraction. One additional value to super-types and sub-types is that we can specify relationships at either level to gain a more precise picture of the relationships being modeled.

For example, in the data model below the super-type entity **Animal** is related to **Reproduction Season**. If we did not have **Animal**, then we would have to relate **Mammal** and **Reptile** and **Fish** to **Reproduction Season**. Further, the **Nesting Site** entity is related to **Mammal** and not to **Reptile** or **Fish**. Finally, the **Body of Water** entity is related to **Fish** only and is not relevant to **Reptile** and **Mammal**:

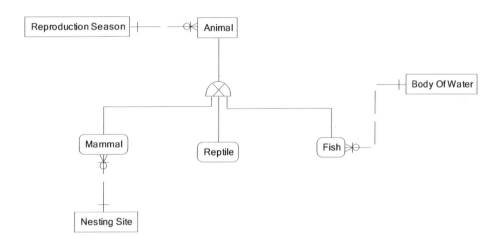

ONE-TO-ONE PEER TO PEER RELATIONSHIPS

There are times when two entities are of equal importance and they have a one to one relationship. This situation is rare, but it does happen, and is frequently modeled incorrectly. Below we allow this IRS database to record information about a person who may or may not have a Social Security number:

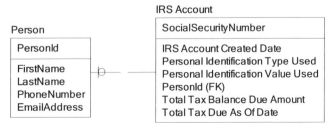

When a person gets assigned a Social Security number, a new row is inserted in the IRS Account entity that is linked to the proper Person Id.

Key Points

- The classification of the things around us into categories allows us to make behavioral generalizations, which, while not always true, will be true often enough to give us lots of value.

- One-to-one relationships between entities exist that are not classification hierarchies (peer to peer relationships above). These are surprisingly frequently missed by data modelers.

Modeling Time and Historical Events

The conceptual data model may or may not model the history of data values changing over time. Most CDMs model the current state of an entity without regard to the state of data in the past. The exceptions would be systems that have stringent requirements around tracking history. For example, banking applications are highly oriented to tracking history, so they would have historical entities in their CDM. Systems that are less attuned to history, such as instant messaging systems, will have fewer entities dedicated to historical tracking, and the CDM may ignore history completely.

The logical data model and physical data model for all systems will articulate the places where history is required to be tracked. Again, some systems have very few requirements to track history and would have few historical entities and attributes in their LDM and PDM. This is rare since most systems have several historical tracking requirements.

When modeling history, there will be two types of entities. First are "static entities" that do not change over time. Second are "dynamic entities" that do change over time

STATIC ENTITIES
Static entities are the anchor points for their neighbor entities that have the purpose of tracking changes over time for some aspect of the anchor entity. For example, **Person** has these unchanging attributes:

- Birth date
- Birth location
- Biological mother
- Biological father

And **Building** has these unchanging attributes:

- Date occupancy permit granted

- City
- State

DYNAMIC HISTORICAL ENTITIES

Associated to each static or anchor entity will be entities that track change over time for a particular type of change. For example, **Person** has these dynamic entities:

- Job History
- Marriage History
- Residence History
- Health History
- Hobby History

And Building these dynamic entities:

- Remodel History
- Cleaning History
- Handicap Access Upgrade History
- Landscape Upgrade History

In the logical data model, the history entities typically have a natural key that includes the date and time of the event being tracked. Some history entities include both the start date and time and the end date and time of the event being tracked, so the interval of the chunk of time is clearly known. Further, the granularity of time varies for each type of historical event. Fine-grain time units would be nanoseconds or milliseconds. Coarse-grain time units would be months or years. Different historical event types will have different time granularities:

- Date only for 24-hour granularity, for example Wedding Date
- Date and time to the minute, for example Contract Signed Time
- Date and time to the millisecond, for example Network Packet Delay

Below are examples of **Person** anchor, history entities, and date attributes:

- Employment History has Employment Start Date and Employment End Date
- Marriage History has Marriage Start Date and Marriage End Date
- Residence History has Residence Start Date and Residence End Date
- Health History has Test Date and Time, Diagnosis Date and Time, and Surgery Date and Time
- Hobby History has Hobby Start Date and Hobby End Date

And examples of **Building** anchor, history entities, and date attributes:

- Remodel History has Remodel Start Date and Remodel End Date
- Cleaning History has Cleaning Date
- Handicap Access Upgrade History has Handicap Access Upgrade Start Date and Time and Handicap Access Upgrade End Date and Time
- Landscape Upgrade History has Landscape Upgrade Start Date and Landscape Upgrade End Date

Standard data modeling rules for uniqueness are applied by comparing primary key values in the rows to detect duplicates. When date ranges become part of the uniqueness criteria, we must add application logic to detect intersecting date and time ranges. This logic is an extension of the traditional data value uniqueness criteria. Therefore, when we include date ranges to track history with start and end dates, we need to use application logic to maintain the uniqueness of rows.

Uniqueness that relies on application code is bad for system complexity and maintainability. But with no declarative database date range options, we must rely on programmer-developed logic to enforce most of the rules for historical databases. There are three basic types of date ranges:

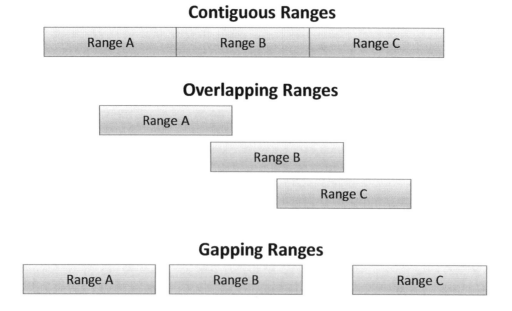

In contiguous date ranges, the end of "Range A" is one unit of time before the start of "Range B". For example, if **Marriage** is tracked by minute, then my divorce must be complete one minute before my next marriage can be started (example is contiguous to the minute):

- Marriage A–End Date Time = Jan 1, 2010, 1:01 PM
- Marriage B–Start Date Time = Jan 1, 2010, 1:02 PM

In overlapping date ranges, "Range A" can end after the start of "Range B". If **Marriage** allows polygamy, then my divorce for "marriage A" need not be complete before my "marriage B" can start (example shows one minute of polygamy):

- Marriage A–End Date Time = Jan 1, 2010, 1:01 PM
- Marriage B–Start Date Time = Jan 1, 2010, 1:00 PM

In gapping date ranges, the end of "Range A" can have a gap before the start of "Range B". If **Marriage** allows for people to be unmarried for a period of time, which happens, then the end of one marriage can have a gap before the start of the next marriage

- Marriage A–End Date Time = Jan 1, 2010, 1:01 PM
- Marriage B–Start Date Time = Sept 26, 2012, 3:00 PM

Below is an example with data that uses a range type of contiguous for all history entities. This means that a person's employment history can have no gaps. This is a hypothetical design, since in reality, people may have employment gaps.

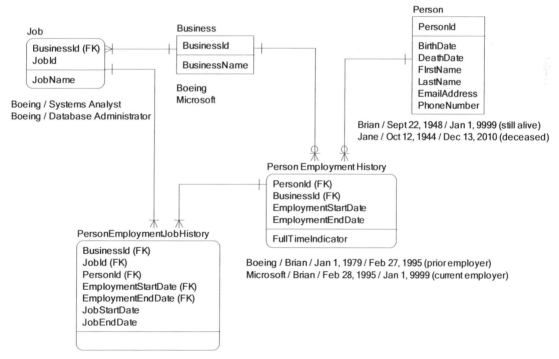

Boeing / Brian / Jan 1, 1979 / Feb 27, 1995 / Jan 1, 1979 / March 12, 1982 / Systems Analyst
Boeing / Brian / Jan 1, 1979 / Feb 27, 1995 / March 13, 1982 / Feb 27, 1995 / Database Administrator

Traditional referential integrity rules between a primary key and the related foreign keys have extra logic for historical data referential integrity. Traditional referential integrity would enforce that each row in **PersonEmploymentHistory** already exists in **Person** before creating a new row in **PersonEmploymentHistory**. Now, when we are dealing with history tables, there is one additional referential integrity check to ensure that the **PersonEmploymentHistory** date ranges fall between the **Person** attributes of BirthDate and DeathDate.

In common sense language, we need to ensure that every person must be employed between the person's birth date and death date. We only employ living people. Again, this self-evident rule is difficult to implement in most physical databases.

The next level of date range referential integrity rule deals with the entity **PersonEmploymentJobHistory**. This entity tracks the jobs that a person does when that person is employed by a business. Further, all rows in **PersonEmploymentJobHistory** must exist during the date ranges in **PersonEmploymentHistory**.

If I worked for a business called `Boeing` between `Jan 1, 2000` and `Jan 1 2010`, then all my rows in **PersonEmploymentJobHistory** for me at Boeing must exist during the date ranges of Jan 1, 2000 and Jan 1, 2010, which is the time I was employed at Boeing. In common sense language, all job history rows for a given person in a given business must happen during that person's employment at that business. No surprises here, but again, believe it or not, most databases do not support this obvious rule easily.

I asked Luke if he had any questions about the three types of date ranges or date range referential integrity. Luke suddenly looked confused and said, "Can't we have date range rules that combine more than one of the three types of range rules?" Again, I was startled to find his thinking to be so perceptive. I replied, "Yes, in the real world there are history rules that use multiple range types to enforce uniqueness."

To make the point, I hopped onto my data modeling tool and pounded out this example, which uses both contiguous and gapping referential integrity history range types. Brian's first marriage was contiguous with his second marriage. Brian's second marriage was gapping with his third marriage:

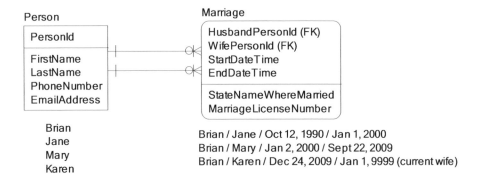

Key Points

- The passage of time is such an integral aspect of our awareness that it is hard to imagine that most database management systems do a poor job of implementing historical data requirements. Additionally, data modeling of time is often ignored or designed inconsistently.

- We have design techniques for specification of history requirements in data models that are consistent and expressive. For implementation of history in physical databases, get ready to work hard.

Normalization

Normalization theory was originally created by mathematicians to guide database designers in how to conform to the set operation rules of the Structured Query Language (SQL) and how to avoid update anomalies. The theory eliminated redundancy of attributes, making updates easy since each fact resided in one and only one place. Each fact also had the exact unique key to give it a distinct context.

For example, the fact called Shoe Size 12D is more meaningful when you know it belongs to a given individual. Note the exception to "no redundancy" is the propagation of primary keys from one entity to another entity as a foreign key. This PK-FK redundancy is mostly managed by the referential integrity rules of database management systems.

The theory of normalization has been expressed in non-mathematical terms many times. The contents and implications of this theory vary widely between most non-mathematical presentations. These pragmatic interpretations of normalization theory present valuable insights into data modeling design principles. No single normalization interpretation is the whole truth of good data model design. I will present my own flavor of a pragmatic interpretation of normalization theory that aligns closely with *Extended Relational Analysis*.

Entities have attributes that identify unique instances of the entity, and other attributes that describe each instance of the entity. Any given attribute is either part of the entity's primary key, or is a descriptive or non-primary-key attribute. Normalization theory guides us in designing which descriptive attributes belong in a given entity.

First, we must design the primary key of the entity to determine the uniqueness of rows. Second, we must design the set of descriptive Attributes that belong in the entity along with the primary key. Third, we must look for multiple uniqueness constraints beyond the primary key and document those alternate keys. Finally, we can take one last look at the non-key attributes to see if they belong in the entity considering the alternate keys.

Normalization theory will state that Attribute X is dependent on Attribute Y. The phrase "is dependent on" would be more clearly stated as "is uniquely identified by." Normalization rules state, for example:

- Tax Amount Due is dependent on Social Security Number and Filing Year
- Person Skill Level is dependent on Hobby Identifier and Social Security Number

Which translated into clear language:

- Tax Amount Due is uniquely identified by Social Security Number and Filing Year
- Person Skill Level is uniquely identified by Hobby Identifier and Social Security Number

FIRST NORMAL FORM

First normal form means all attributes are atomic and not repeating. Each attribute contains atomic data. Atomic data is a collection of data that is acted on as a unit. Example, in the **Person** entity, the Full Name attribute should be changed to be the attributes First Name and Last Name to conform to first normal form. Searching for a first name that equals `Jean Luc` is hard when we store the Full Name, since there can be different people with names like:

- First Name = `Jean Luc` and Last Name = `Ponty`
- First Name = `Jean` and Last Name = `Luc Ponty`

When we tell the database about the atomic components of compound things, then the database can properly understand them. If we hide the atomic components of compound things, then developers need to guess where the boundaries were intended to exist, which is a bad choice. No attribute is repeated. For example, in the **Person** entity, attributes Hobby1, Hobby2, Hobby3 would be a repeating group and violate first normal form. Alternatively, the attribute Hobbies List, with a list of hobbies separated by commas, is also a violation of first normal form, as it is a repeating group, too. **Hobby** belongs in a new entity that is outside of the **Person** entity.

SECOND NORMAL FORM

Second normal form means attributes can't be dependent on a subset of the key. An entity is in second normal form when it is in first normal form and no non-primary-key attributes depend on a subset of the key. Second normal form only applies to entities with compound primary keys or with compound alternate keys. If an entity has a single attribute primary key and single attribute alternate keys, then second normal form does not apply. Example:

An entity called **Person Hobby** has a compound primary key consisting of Person Id and Hobby Id. If I put an attribute into **Person Hobby** called Last Name, I have violated second normal form, since Last Name depends on PersonId, and PersonId is only half of the primary key. Last Name is not dependent on HobbyId. The example below is a violation of second normal form:

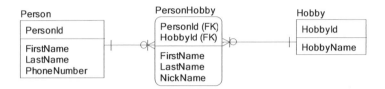

In the entity **Person Hobby**, the attributes First Name and Last Name are a violation of second normal form since they are uniquely identified by a subset of the PK called Person Id. Further, if someone updated their Last Name in the **Person** entity and forgot to update their Last Name in the **Person Hobby** entity, then we would have an update anomaly. When the database is in a contradictory state, different people can think I have different last names, when in reality I only have one current last name.

The attribute Nickname in the entity **Person Hobby** is not a violation, since I allow each person to change his or her nickname for each hobby. When I play tennis with my brother, he prefers the nickname `Racketman`, and when I play soccer with my brother he prefers the nickname `Hot Shot`.

THIRD NORMAL FORM

Third normal form means attributes cannot be dependent on a superset of the key. An entity is in third normal form when it is in both first and second normal forms and no attributes of the entity are dependent on non-primary key attributes for their meaning. For example, the entity **Employee** below has a primary key of Employee Id. The entity also contains non-primary key attributes of Salary Type and Salary Dollar Amount. Salary Type can be either hourly or salaried. Salary Dollar Amount will contain rows with values like $15.00, $14.00, $22.00, $47,000, $57,555. Not surprisingly, when rows of data have a group in the teens and twenties and another group of values in the tens of thousands, you suspect the column is serving multiple purposes. Further, set operations on the attribute Salary Dollar Amount would be meaningless across the two salary types of hourly and salaried, especially when it is time to calculate paychecks.

Employee

Employeeld
FirstName
LastName
WorkDepartmentName
SalaryType
SalaryDollarAmount

Brian / Shive / DB Department / Hourly / $22.00
Bill / Gates / Executive / Salaried / $225,000.00

Salary Amount depends on both the Employee Id and the Salary Type. Since Salary Type is outside of the primary key, this is violation of third normal form.

To fix this example so that it conforms to third normal form requires us to add two new entities called **Salaried Employee** and **Hourly Employee**:

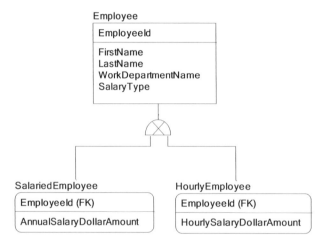

These two new entities are sub-types of the super-type entity of **Employee**. A one-to-one relationship exists between **Employee** and both **Salaried Employee** and **Hourly Employee**.

Now we can do meaningful entity-wide set operations on the attribute AnnualSalaryDollarAmount in **Salaried Employee**, and on the attribute HourlySalaryDollarAmount in **Hourly Employee**.

NORMALIZATION OF INTERSECTIONS

Many-to-many entities can have two or more identifying relationships in the intersection entity. This topic can be approached under normalization forms beyond the third normal form, but I prefer a simpler approach that has a common sense relationship to discovery over time and minimal relationships. This is yet another use of Occam's Razor.

These intersection entities can also be called *associative entities*. The issue in normalization of intersections is to decide how many identifying relationships to put in each many-to-many entity. Intersection normalization must honor the sequence of knowing things and use as few relationships in an intersection as possible. For example, I am going to start recording my friends and the hobbies they do with me, as well as the locations where we do the hobby and the equipment used to do it. I could choose to track all these relationships in a single intersection entity that represents a four-way intersection, as diagramed on the facing page.

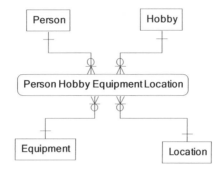

Rarely, if ever, is this correct. This design ignores the sequence of discovery of friends, hobbies, and their relationships. It also uses the maximum set of relationships in the four-way intersection entity, **Person Hobby Equipment Location**. No information can be recorded in the data model about relationships until we know everything.

A better design is to consider that we first come to know a person plays a hobby and would like to capture this fact. Later we will ask about the equipment the person uses or where the person plays the hobby. The sequence is to first meet the person and then find out the person plays a hobby. Then we either know the equipment for the person's hobby or the location where the person plays the hobby, as shown in the following diagram.

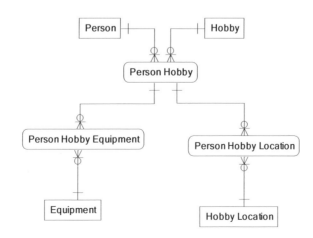

Later we discover that there may be special sports where a single hobby uses different equipment based on the location where it is being played. In this case, we must add a fact (**Person Hobby Equipment Location**) that is uncovered last in the sequence of fact discovery, as shown in the diagram on the next page. It will be populated rarely since most hobbies use identical equipment for all locations.

Luke was totally burned out after my diatribe on normalization, as was I. He missed at least half the ideas, but when we go to actually build his database to run his business, we would revisit these normalization concepts.

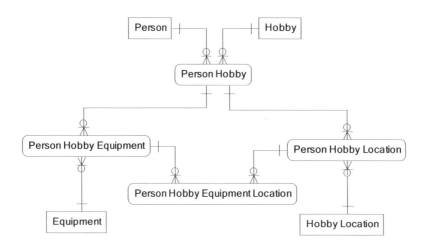

Before we launched into the final topic, we went to the beach to play in the sand and watch the waves crash into themselves. The ocean tends to clear out the mind and make space for new ideas to take root. I got sunburn while Luke, with his darker skin, played in the sun all day and showed few signs of overexposure.

Key Points

- Normalization is an important set of rules that constrain how logical data models are designed.

- Like the jazz musician, sitar player, and sports star in the zone, we have our data model rules, and yet we have an astronomic free space for creativity.

- Learn the rules, follow the rules, yet be creative. Structure and creativity are both needed for good designing.

Master Data, Transactional Data, and Measurement Data

When we returned, the final new idea for data modeling would be presented to a refreshed and ready-to-learn Luke. The final lesson was the distinction between master data, transactional data, and measurements of the world.

Master data is highly shared across processes and users. It is generally created by a small group and is viewed by a large group. Examples include: Product, Customer, Date, Sales Status, Order Status and Billing Status.

Transactional data is narrowly shared across processes and users. It is generally created by a large group, but it is viewed by a small group who are associated with the transaction. Very few processes and users can view transactional data, such as:

- Contract (I can't see your contract)
- Order (I can't see your order)
- Invoice (I would like to give you my invoice to pay it, but you refuse)
- Return (I would like to return your product for a refund to me, but can't)

Measurement data is master and transactional data transformed for metrics. Measurement data is used by those needing to evaluate the success or failure of some aspect of the business, such as for **Point of Sale Fact** examples are Customer Dimension, Product Dimension, Time Dimension, and Store Dimension.

When looking at a data model, look for entities that are either master, transactional, or measurement. For example, in the following data model there are subject area boxes around the entities for master data, transactional data and measurement data.

I added sample data intended to quickly clarify the meaning of this restaurant data model. It is intended to clarify the distinctions between master data, transactional data, and measurement data:

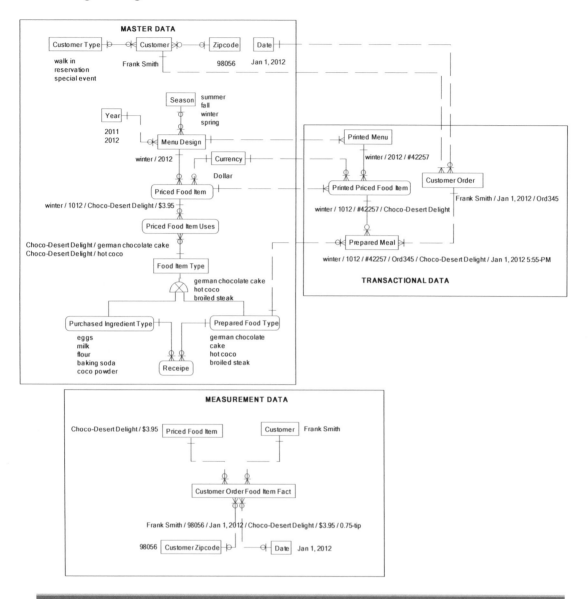

Key Points

- Conceptual, logical, and physical data designs are best understood when the contents of the designs are categorized by master data, transactional data, and measurement data. Often, data models will mix master, transactional, and measurement data without clearly identifying these categories.

- This three-way categorization brings clarity to the semantic value of the models, as well as uniting the thinking of diverse participants in the business and IT.

Chapter 6
Luke's Lemons, Inc. Business and Data Model

Season #1 Business Plan

Luke's first season in the lemon business was pretty tough. His toy purchases dropped off precipitously, and his free time did the same. His first mistake was in hiring his Xbox friends as employees. They were fifth and sixth graders, but the concept "work" was not well known to either of them. Secondly, Luke failed to specify roles and responsibilities. This led to frequent arguments over what is "fair" and what is "not fair." Below is the value chain model for Season One.

CONCEPTUAL VALUE CHAIN MODEL

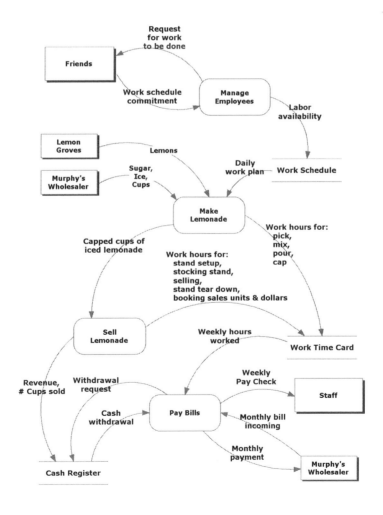

This first season's business model is pretty simple. The three boys pick lemons, make juice, and sell it on three different street corners. The lemons and water are free and the sugar, ice, and cups are purchased at wholesale prices. Each weekend, Luke visits his two friends, Cyrus and Aden, pays them for the prior week, and then arranges for the next week's work schedule. Workers are paid a fixed amount per hour. The pay rate in the first season was $7.25 per hour. Luke's friend Cyrus lives near the Murphy's wholesale warehouse, so he picks up sugar, ice, and cups each workday morning. Murphy's sends a bill at month's end.

CONCEPTUAL DATA MODEL

Below are the "things of interest" to Luke's business from the viewpoint of the business owner—in this case, Luke himself. There are entities of interest, relationships of interest, and attributes of interest.

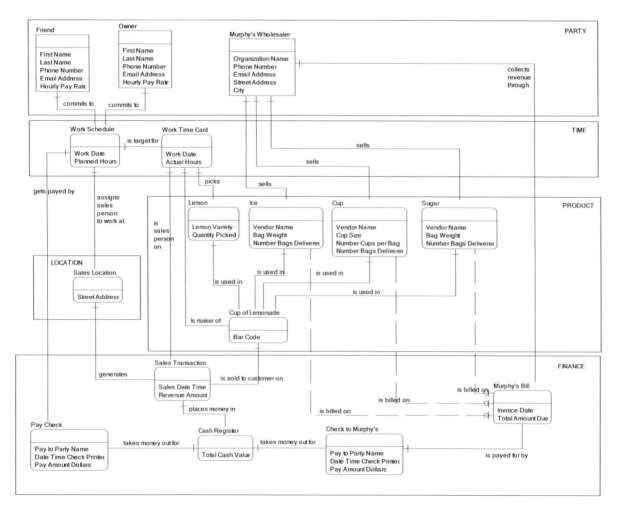

Above is the CDM with a few of the major attributes included to give it more meaning. Uniqueness constraints do not belong in a CDM, so they are blank. Further, CDM attributes do not conform to normalization theory.

LOGICAL DATA MODEL

Logical data models do not specify any particular technologies - we could implement the models below with a relational database, or we could use pencil and paper. Sample data values are displayed to indicate some of the data values that might reside inside of the entities.

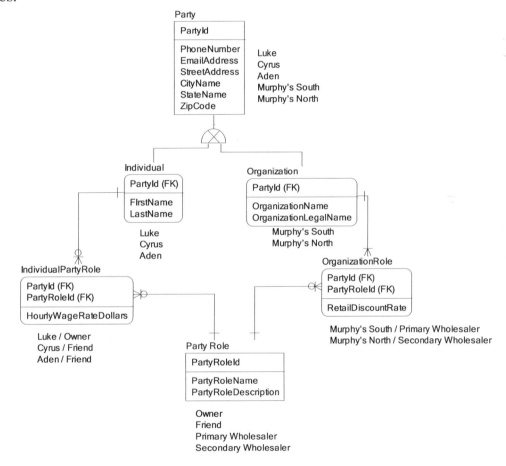

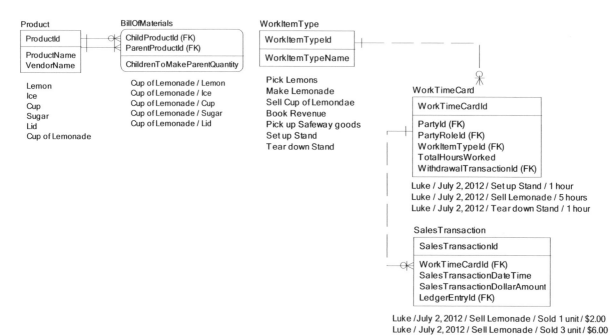

Here is the entire LDM for Season #1 (entity only level shown for readability):

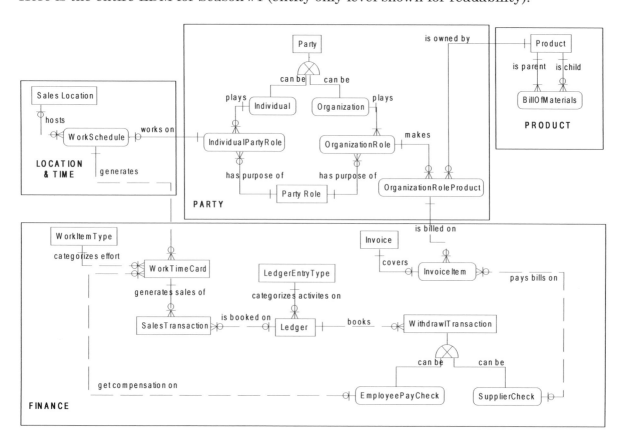

Here is a mapping from a concept to its logical counterparts:

CDM Entity	LDM Entity (most are abstracted for schema stability)
Friend	Party / Individual / Role / Individual Party Role
Owner	Party / Individual / Role / Individual Party Role
Murphy's Wholesaler	Party / Organization / Role / Organization Role
Work Schedule	Work Schedule
Work Time Card	Work Time Card
Lemon	Product / Bill of Materials
Ice	Product / Bill of Materials
Cup	Product / Bill of Materials
Sugar	Product / Bill of Materials
Cup of Lemonade	Product / Bill of Materials
Sales Location	Sales Location
Sales Transaction	Sales Transaction
Pay Check	Withdrawal Transaction / Employee Pay Check
Cash Register	Ledger
Check to Murphy's	Withdrawal Transaction / Supplier Check
Murphy's Bill	Invoice / Invoice Item

Here is a description of each of the relationships:

- A party can be either an individual or an organization.
- Party roles define the purpose of both individuals and organizations.
- An individual party playing a role can commit to a work schedule.
- An organization party playing a role can deliver products (raw materials such as ice, sugar, cups).
- A product is composed of a collection of component products that, when assembled, create the finished goods product.
- A work schedule generates work time card entries that describe what work was actually done during that scheduled work period.
- The work item type describes the nature of the work being performed.
- A work time card can generate revenue on sales transactions.
- Each ledger entry is categorized by a ledger entry type.
- Sales transactions are booked on a ledger.
- The ledger records withdrawal transactions.
- Withdrawal transactions can be for either an employee paycheck or a supplier payment.

Here is a description of each of the entities in the Party subject area:

- **Party**–either an individual or an organization
- **Individual**–a person who has or will participate in the business
- **Organization**–a legal entity that has or will participate in the business
- **Party Role**–the set of purposes that parties may have
- **Individual Party Role**–the purpose of a person
- **Organization Party Role**–the purpose of a legal entity
- **Organization Role Product**–the set of products produced by an organization

And a description of each of the entities in the Product subject area:

- **Product**–the thing being sold (finished goods) or some component of the thing being sold (component as work in progress)
- **Bill of Materials**–the list of component products needed to build finished goods

And a description of each of the entities in the Location and Time subject area:

- **Sales Location**–the place where the lemonade stand resides
- **Work Schedule**–the time and place that a person will work at a lemonade stand

And a description of each of the entities in the Finance subject area:

- **Work Item Type**–a categorization of the type of effort that a person is doing during his work time
- **Work Time Card**–a record of who worked for how long doing which work item type
- **Sales Transaction**–the event that exchanges finished goods for money and records the revenue in the ledger
- **Ledger Entry Type**–a categorization of the reasons for recording financial transactions
- **Ledger**–the place where financial transactions are stored
- **Withdrawal Transactions**–the event that pays either our employees or our partners who supply us with goods and services

PHYSICAL DATA MODEL

The physical model was being implemented on SQL Server. With the logical data model complete, we only needed to alter the PDM physical model to take advantage of the strengths of SQL Server and avoid its weaknesses. In this case, we changed the LDM subtypes under **Withdrawal Transaction** to be one to one relationships, since SQL Server has no declarative relationship for sub-types.

Note that in relational database systems the designer of the database can execute a single command to declare relationship rules called "referential integrity" rules. Then all processes that execute against the system inherit this rule, with no exceptions.

Next we dropped the LDM Party entity and moved the LDM attributes of Party redundantly into the PDM Individual table and into the PDM Organization tables. For example, the Party entity in the LDM had attributes of phone number, email address, and street address. Now these attributes have been copied to both the PDM Individual table and the PDM Organization table.

This should have been a high profit margin business since the lemons were all free, but an unusually rainy summer cast a dark shadow on demand for lemonade. In addition, Luke's employees got $7.25 per hour and goofed off for at least half of their working time, making their effective pay rate $14.50 per hour.

The seasons and the earth would produce new fruit next year for Luke, an older and wiser entrepreneur. Luke would grow profitability next season with some geriatric ideas from dad and our best friend and neighbor, Trudy.

Season #2 Business Plan

In Luke's second season he was determined to avoid the pitfalls of his prior season. He reminded me that this season he will get some tips from dad. And these tips were to be specific to the lemon business on our property in our times (no more philosophy for Luke). We called in Trudy, our next door neighbor and best friend, for her consulting on how Luke's Lemons Season #2 could bear more financial fruits than the dreaded Season #1.

Trudy and Luke play lots of creative games together and laugh quite a bit. One of their games is called "stuffies," where they take stuffed animals and put on plays, play games, and invent a community of characters that have a blast every minute. Trudy suggested we put on a play called "last summer's lemon business." Then after the play was over, we could sit and talk about how the characters and plot can change for next year's efforts.

- I played the customers who were thirsty and in a hurry, as played by a giraffe and a penguin.
- Trudy played Luke, the boss of the business, as played by a lion and a mouse.
- Luke played his friend Aden, who had a tough summer with little money and less time, as played by a teddy bear.

As the play got started, the "boss" kept alternating between strength (lion) and fearfulness (mouse). This allowed the workers to goof off several hours per day, and then when the "boss" morphed back to the lion, it triggered some actual work to get done.

Luke complained that Trudy's character in the play was doing a disservice to his actual leadership skills. Both Trudy and dad agreed that reality and the play were highly aligned on this issue. Suddenly Luke announced that the play should stop. He tried again to revise history and claim strong leadership last summer, and then he started fishing for a way to have the workers lead themselves. Trudy grabbed her Post-It note and jotted down what would become "Tip #1 for Season #2."

We resumed the play with a brief detour, as the animals spontaneously digressed into *Star Wars* followed by ninja warriors. As the play slowly morphed back to the original plot, the workers at Luke's Lemons were complaining more and more. At one point, the bear, lion, and mouse were in a free-for-all wrestling match that caused collateral damage to the giraffe while he was trying to pay for his drink. Again Trudy scribbled a cryptic note, and, voilà, "Tip #2 for Season #2" was born.

As the stuffed animal play decayed in to a Three Stooges' pie throwing contest, Trudy suggested we talk about next summer for a few minutes. We spent the next half hour brainstorming ideas for improving next summer. We used Post-It notes and a whiteboard; all ideas were respected and given a fair evaluation. The two winning ideas to be implemented next summer for Season #2 were as follows:

- Tip one was that each person should earn pay according to their sales. Each person would get an attribute called "Percent of Revenue as Wages." The revenue not going to wages would be used as cash on hand for future business needs.
- Tip two was that each employee should understand both the value chain model and the data model and identify his responsibility on the models. This way there would be no confusion about each person's roles and responsibilities.

This new business model takes care of employee motivation and employee education. People's paychecks will be proportionate to their sales success. This avoids the employees goofing off half the time while getting paid full time. People's understanding of where they fit in the value chain will be explicit, understood, and agreed to by all. This avoids the arguments about "Hey, dude, that's not fair."

I reminded Luke that he also gets a computing system in Season #2. Luke seemed uninterested in a computer with no games loaded. I reminded him that profitability and information management are strongly linked. We started with changes to the Season #1 CDM.

CONCEPTUAL VALUE CHAIN MODEL

In Season #1 Luke paid employees based on hours worked. In Season #2, he will be paying employees by a percent of their revenue generated on sales. So, while the value chain model at "level one" stays the same, there are changes to the calculation of paychecks for employees at the detail process level. In addition, we will remove the CDM attribute called Hourly Pay Rate and replace it with an attribute called Percent Revenue as Wages.

Next we will change the employee paycheck calculation from hourly to the following: In **Sales Transaction**, add up all revenue amounts for a given employee for a given week. Next, multiply that number by the Percent Revenue as Wages to determine the pay check pay amount dollars.

Luke wants to change employee assignments to be ready for Season #2. Last season Cyrus did all the work of going to Murphy's and picking up the ice, sugar, and cups. He did not mind last season, since he got paid for every hour of this effort. Now Cyrus is rightfully complaining that next season he will be doing this work for no pay while other employees will use ice, sugar, and cups that he brought to them.

When presented with this situation, the boss, Luke, decided that each employee would take turns going to Murphy's to pick up ice, sugar, and cups. This distributes the hours spent at Murphy's evenly across all employees. Luke even offered to take his turn going to Murphy's so that he would also absorb his fair share of this unpaid time. Finally, Luke needed to train each employee in the value chain process and make clear where they were responsible for taking action.

For Season #2, the data flow diagram of the value chain will be coded with who does what in the value chain. This documentation will be of value when arguments arise over who is doing how much work. The diagram on the facing page is Season #2 DFD with responsibilities marked with asterisks.

Since Trudy works in the medical field, where proper process and data flow can mean life or death, I asked her to train the boys on how to read a value chain data flow diagram. The boys were glad to have a new face teaching them about businesses and computing systems. Last season, each employee kept their own work plan on their personal calendar. This turned into the classic nightmare of storing data that is hidden from others in the value chain. Cyrus would update his work schedule and not tell the others. Then Luke and Aden would be waiting for Cyrus to come with the ice and he never showed up. Cyrus' schedule was updated to reflect his fishing trip, but Luke and Aden never saw his schedule update.

All three boys agreed that Luke should collect labor availability schedules and publish the daily work plan each night to describe the coming work day. A phone call from Luke to Cyrus and Aden would make sure the next day's schedule contained minimum surprises.

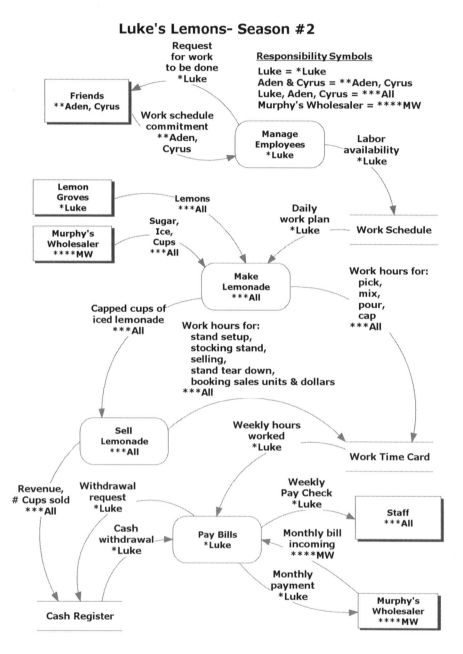

Luke's Lemons- Season #2

Responsibility Symbols

Luke = *Luke
Aden & Cyrus = **Aden, Cyrus
Luke, Aden, Cyrus = ***All
Murphy's Wholesaler = ****MW

CONCEPTUAL DATA MODEL

Here is the updated CDM:

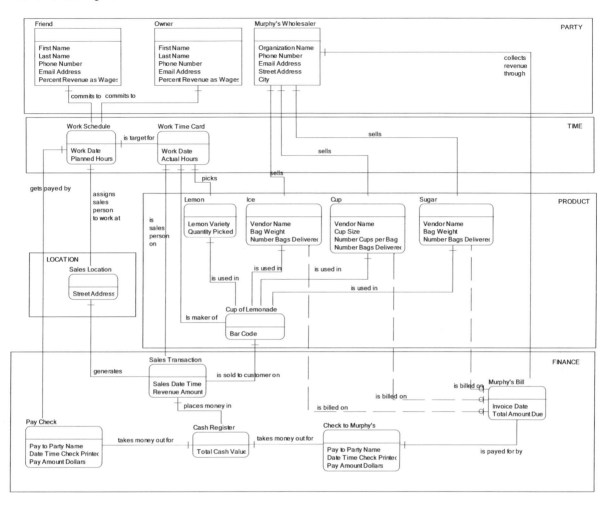

LOGICAL DATA MODEL

The LDM changes mirror the CDM changes closely. Hourly wage rate was removed and percent revenue as wages was added. The revenue that does not go to wages is added to the business's cash on hand. This would allow next season's business model to invest heavily in partners and sales.

When Cyrus and Aden saw the sample data, they were shocked at Luke's 70% portion of his sales. Luke pointed out that this was just sample data in a CDM training course and the final values would land in the real computer system that dad was going to build before next summer.

Cyrus and Aden were not calmed by Luke's assertion that final percentages were yet to be determined. They whimpered in unison "That's not fair!" and Aden proclaimed that they should get 70% of their sales and Luke should get 55%.

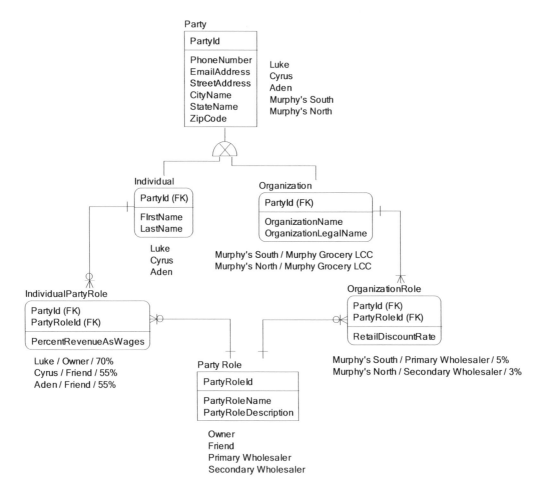

Trudy spotted a chance to resolve anger and conflict with some value chain thinking. She returned to the Season #2 DFD where the job responsibilities were marked with asterisks. She walked through a typical week and the people doing work had to stand during that part of their work description. Luke was standing almost the entire time. Aden and Cyrus were sitting more often than they might have expected.

Both Cyrus and Aden started to be sympathetic to the effort required to manage schedules, collect money, calculate paychecks for employees, pay Murphy's, and manage all the squabbles that erupt daily, on top of picking lemons, squeezing, making lemonade, setting up the stand, selling, and tearing down the stand.

When Cyrus and Aden more fully appreciated the extra effort Luke was making, they looked at 70% as a plausible number for Luke next season. The value chain training was paying off already:

- Cooperation and teamwork was expanding as conflict and anger subsided. Understanding the larger context in which the entire team operates gives members an objective framework for discussion and compromise.
- Different brains that store the same value chain model become less divisive.
- Having a single paradigm to describe the business is good. Teaching this single paradigm to all participants is great!

PHYSICAL DATA MODEL

The changes to the PDM are exactly like the changes to the LDM. The column hourly pay rate was removed and the column percent revenue as wages was added. The business logical that physically calculates employee paycheck amount needs to be changed to reflect the new revenue sharing logic.

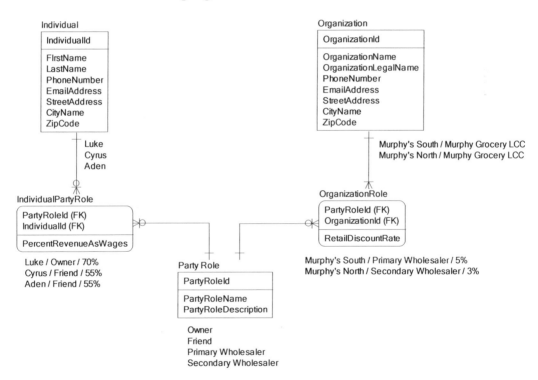

Trudy was looking at the data model above and wondered how the database design keeps us from having two party roles called "Owner." We want one and only one party role called "Owner," and that row called "Owner" has one description called "The person who manages the business and all finances." Luke chimed in and wondered how the database design keeps us from having two party role descriptions that both read "The person who manages the business and all finances."

These were both good questions since the PDM diagram above shows one uniqueness constraint on Party Role Id, and that value is assigned by SQL Server with a new value on every insert. This allows the following rows of data to be inserted to the table Party Role:

Party Role Id	Party Role Name	Party Role Description
1	Owner	The person who manages the business and all finances.
2	Owner	The person who dumps the trash and sweeps the floors
3	Friend	The person who manages the business and all finances.

What the database diagram did not show are the alternate keys for uniqueness. The diagram showed only the primary key that is the column Party Role Id that is a system assigned key. There exist two more uniqueness constraints that are natural keys for uniqueness. These natural business keys are defined by the business. Aden jumped in and said that the table **Individual** suffers from the same problem in that the following rows can exist as documented by the database design diagram:

Individual Id	First Name	Last Name	Phone Number	Email Address
1	Aden	Jones	206 345-2525	ZZRyder@live.com
2	Aden	Jones	206 345-2525	ZZRyder@live.com
3	Cyrus	Nimmo	425 455-6870	CyGuy@live.com

I opened my data modeling program and printed out the PDM with the AK option turned on. It looked like the diagram below and addresses all the uniqueness concerns (see the model on the facing page).

The table **Party Role** has three unique indexes: one primary key on Party Role Id, one alternate key on **Partly Role Name**, and another alternate key on **Party Role Description**. **Individual** requires all of the descriptive attributes for uniqueness and **Organization** requires all but one descriptive attribute for uniqueness.

After a few hot days of selling near the local parade and fair, the thought of earning $88 in a single day was nirvana. When nirvana materializes in your wallet, your attitude can mellow without much effort. The boys worked hard, and each earned over $1,400. They were not only enjoying the fruits of their lemon labor (games, trips, bikes), but they were also developing the positive feelings that come from the virtuous cycle of plan, work, and measure—and then suddenly you have over a thousand dollars.

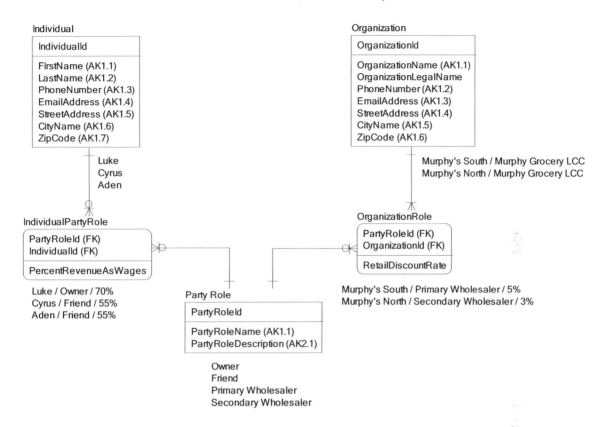

Luke's Lemons business had $2,100 in cash on hand after Season #2. The feeling of "work begets success" needs to become ingrained in youth to stick well. The boys had grown significantly from last season's bickering, shouting, and minimum wage summer. Things like getting along, working together, compromise, hard work, and the fruits of reward at the end of work are things that are hard to learn as an adult and come naturally to boys and young men. I was in Boy Scouts for years and found many of these same skills emerge naturally from participation in Scouting activities. I was an Eagle Scout, Boy Scout Master, and worked as a District Executive for the Boy Scouts.

I will get Luke involved with Boy Scouts as soon as he reaches age 11. He has already announced his protest about camping and hiking. Too bad for him; he will learn to grow in the lemon business, and then he will learn to grow some more in Scouting.

The computing system I built for Luke was tolerated by the boys at first. It was "uncool" to be seen using my system. But when the cash started coming in large waves, the computational power of our computing system was clearly saving them hours and hours of work. My friend Scott did the user interface, and I did the database work. It wasn't pretty, but it did the job.

At the end of Season #2, the boys all agreed that dad's little IT system was "surprisingly valuable." I am pretty sure that Gutenberg's children found the printing press to be "surprisingly valuable" as well. We had a few basic queries that ran on the database to track the progress of the business. Next season, we would take the database and transform it into a business intelligence structure of facts and dimensions. This would open the doors to hundreds of meaningful views of reporting. Scott and I are hoping to take our volunteer IT shop beyond the "surprisingly valuable," all the way to just plain valuable.

Season #3 Business Plan

Season #3 would turn out to be highly transformational for Luke's business. In the first two seasons, Luke let over 98% of the lemons go to waste on the ground. In the next season, the waste would drop precipitously and profits would grow nicely. We started planning Season #3 in late October, so I had lots of time to adjust the computing system, and Luke had lots of time to prepare the employees with training.

Last season, Luke really enjoyed the tranquility of operating a business where responsibility was clearly understood and teamwork just seemed to flow. During a severe thunderstorm, Trudy, Luke, and I sat down to start planning the coming summer's business model. I was excited since they had quite a large stash of cash on hand to enlist help with a new summer of selling. Trudy said that in her opinion, the biggest problem was that Luke's business lacked specialization in the division of labor.

When everybody does everything in a business, there is no chance for people to specialize in a task and gain efficiencies from that specialization. Luke, Cyrus, and Aden all do picking, squeezing lemons, mixing sugar, making cups of lemonade, transporting lemonade to the sales site, setting up the sales stand, selling, taking money, recording money, and tearing down the sales stand.

Luke was confused and ambivalent on the topic of specialization, so Trudy used her former part-time jewelry business as the example. Trudy did not operate a mine digging for silver and gold, and she did not rock-hunt semi-precious stones. Further, Trudy did not operate a smelter to melt the metal into chains, earrings, rings, and bracelets. Trudy did not polish and cut the stones into shapes suitable for jewelry. What Trudy did do was to purchase the chains, rings, and stones and combine them in new ways to create jewelry. Finally, Trudy sold the jewelry at the annual jewelry exposition and at the monthly county auction.

The lesson here was that Trudy did not have to learn mining, smelting, rock hunting, and rock shaping. Also, she did not have to organize a jewelry exposition or the monthly county auctions. She did, however, combine the works of other specialists in unique ways to create her jewelry. Luke got the principle and applied it immediately. He had been playing with his new friends, Jose and Manuel, at the county park. Their family's truck broke down just outside of town, and they were camping in the park.

Luke knew that Jose and Manuel had parents who specialized in picking fruit although they don't have green cards. Without green cards they work only the harvest season, but the boys said they would be back next July to pick oranges in the southern part of the county. The kids were always looking for small jobs while the parents picked the large crops. Luke said he would ask if they could pick next summer's lemon crop and, if so, how much they would charge.

Next it was my turn to apply Trudy's lesson. The local soda factory was scheduled to be shut down in May. The Koch Soda Company was opening a plant in Mexico. All the current workers were to be fired, and their jobs were being shipped off to cheaper labor markets. The brothers who owned the Koch Soda Company viewed themselves as loyal Americans who were working hard to build a better America for our children and grandchildren. We all look in the mirror and see a rosy version of our true less-than-rosy colored nature. The workers at the Koch plant were collecting money to buy the equipment at the auction. They were also negotiating to rent the plant. The equipment sale price and the building rent would certainly be very low, since empty factory buildings were commonplace in our ailing economy.

I promised to contact the soon-to-be former Koch workers and see if they would like to produce cans of lemonade for us next summer. It would not be a large contract, but several small contracts could keep the factory busy enough to remain viable. The workers hoped to keep the plant open for at least a year while they looked for other jobs.

As the rain stopped, we decided that a bike trip to the park would be fun, so off we went to see the fall tree colors and feel the last warm breeze before winter arrives. During our bike trip, Luke said we should stop so we could talk. He had just figured out that if Jose and Manuel's family pick huge amounts of lemons, and if the former Koch factory produces thousands of cans of lemonade, how could he and Cyrus and Aden sell this gargantuan supply of lemonade?

We were standing near the canoe rental stand and decided to take a canoe trip and discuss the mismatch between lemon supply and demand in Luke's new business model. We were halfway out into the lake before anybody had a solution that was halfway feasible. Trudy came up with the first real idea from something she had read in the paper. The local baseball team was tearing down a perfectly good stadium and was going to build a "nicer facility" on the property. The government was paying for the majority of the costs, since no business person with a calculator and an accountant would have ever tried such a wasteful project.

The county government would run the vendor refreshment stands in the new stadium next summer. They would staff the refreshment stands with members from the local Boy Scout troops. In exchange, the troops would be able to use the county lake and camping facilities for half price. Trudy knew of my extensive contacts with the Boy Scouts and asked me to find out who in the organization was interacting with the county government. With that name, we could petition that person to promote Luke's Lemonade product line to the county official running the refreshment stands. This idea was great since the baseball stadium crowd consumes huge amounts of refreshments.

Not to be outdone, I strained my neural landscape for connections that could move large volumes of lemonade. After 15 minutes of rowing and thinking, I uncovered a reasonable idea for selling large volumes of lemonade. The builder who added a bedroom to my house has a brother, Mark, who builds the display stands for all the vendors at the fairgrounds stadium. The stadium houses the county fair, quilting show, auto show, and several other major events each summer. Mark knows the manager of the refreshment stands and is best friends with the beer vendor. I promised to contact Mark and see if the beer vendor would like to add lemonade to his offerings in order to appeal to a broader demographic of thirsty people.

The outlook for next summer looked amazing as we biked home into the driveway. In the coming months, many pieces of the puzzle fell into place. Luke landed a contract to provide lemonade to the baseball stadium and signed a smaller contract with the fairgrounds beer vendor. Jose and Manuel agreed to come with their brothers to pick lemons next summer at a high rate of productivity and a low wage. The union members at the soon-to-be-defunct Koch Soda plant agreed to produce cans of lemonade at a fraction of the market price. The new business would be non-union and, as such, charged lower prices. The new company at the former Koch Soda plant will be called "Of, By & For the Workers Incorporated."

What a strange feedback loop of things in this business model! All of them are interrelated, and all of them are part good and part bad. Our brains are built to create bulletproof certainty about good guys and bad guys; it is a challenge to remember that all things are a blend of good and bad.

Below are some aspects of Luke's new business model for Season #3 with a list of the good and bad things:

Low wage illegal Mexican workers pick lemons:

Good things	Bad things
• Lemons picked are used to keep the laid-off Koch workers employed • Luke gets low cost lemon harvest	• Immigration laws are being broken • Illegal workers get insufficient health care, education, and housing

The laid-off workers had their old high paying jobs disappear to Mexico:

Good things	Bad things
• Workers in Mexico get jobs • Mexican workers with jobs buy more exports from America • Consumers of Koch Soda may possibly pay less for their drinks • Owners of Koch Soda will definitely get more profits • Low wages and high productivity of "Of, By & For the Workers Inc." help Luke's business	• The "Of, By & For the Workers Inc." business will most likely not exist a year or two from now. • Outsourcing jobs to maximize profits for people who are already millionaires is a value system that hurts America. If this behavior spreads, it can destroy entire sectors of our economy.

I was starting to redesign Luke's computer system for next season when he announced a change to his business model. The brothers who owned the Koch Soda plant would not be firing the workers who squeeze fruit to make juice. All the Koch workers who mix juice and sugar and can the finished drink will be laid off.

Luke was vehement about not doing business with the Koch family since his best friend's father was losing his job. He was searching high and low for someone who could squeeze juice in the volumes and costs required. His only option was to have the lemons shipped 140 miles to a high cost plant in a neighboring state. This would involve extra time, transportation expense, and the juicing costs would be 40% higher. Luke's anger with the Koch family was understandable. I found them somewhat distasteful in many ways as well, but there was a broader lesson to be learned from this situation.

Our consciousness is usually occupied by a mix of both intuitive and rational thinking. A sign that there is too much intuitive thinking getting into our consciousness is absolute *certainty*. If you are 100% sure that I am bad and you are good, stop for a moment and analyze how it is that I might be a little good and you might be a little bad. If you are 100% sure that I am wrong and you are right, stop for a moment and analyze how it is that I might be a little bit right and you might be a little bit wrong. This step of "stop for a moment and analyze" requires us to be self-conscious of when we are letting our primitive intuitive-thinking brain occupy too many neurons in our consciousness.

Luke jumped in and correctly predicted my suggestion of meditation. He was too young and too squirmy to benefit, so I promised we would not try this again until he was older. Meditation builds a meta-consciousness about normal consciousness to monitor for the presence of thoughts during meditation. This meta-consciousness is used to detect the absence of silence in consciousness during meditation. Meditation physically rewires the brain using neuropeptides to maximize rational thinking's footprint in consciousness. Meditation builds a capacity for consciousness to be conscious of itself. This skill is need if we are to monitor the mix of intuitive and rational thinking in our consciousness. This skill is needed if we are to monitor consciousness for silence during meditation.

It is amazing to me that that we all have the capacity to sit with a silent mind focused on breath, and that this simple activity rewires our caveman brains so that we can function with greater peace and equanimity. Yet we are too busy being certain to take the time to act on the thought, "I should sit with no thoughts."

So what does this mean for Luke's Lemons Season #3? Next season we will:

- Offer meditation and breakfast on Mondays, Wednesdays, and Fridays at Luke's house
- Get to know the brothers who run Koch Soda as people who, like us, are good and bad. Then we will select a vendor to juice lemons based on "rational thinking"
- Monitor our thinking and behavior for signs of certainty in our intuitive thinking
- Openly discuss our intuitive-thinking behaviors using rational-thinking for the discussion and analysis

So we scheduled time to meet with Willard and Francis Koch to get to know them as people and to discuss their outsourcing behavior. When we met with the Koch brothers, we found out that they had just been through an agonizing Alzheimer's death with their mother. Luke had just been through an equally heartbreaking experience losing his grandmother to the same disease. As we discussed the myriad emotions of watching a loved one lose, regain, and then lose completely the capacity to think, we agreed that only those who have experienced Alzheimer's can actually understand the disease. When the topic of Boy Scouts was raised by Luke, the Koch brothers asked how the new summer camp swimming pool was doing. Cyrus had told us it was a total blast, so we reiterated his observation. It came out later that the Koch brothers had donated funds to build swimming pools for both the Boy Scouts and the Girl Scouts. So there were lots of good things about the Koch brothers that Luke had not expected.

But when the topic of outsourcing came up, the Koch brothers were certain that it was "the only option that they could find." The high costs of union labor and benefits were making their soda so expensive that fewer people were buying it. The profit margins were shrinking. They had "no choice". Trudy, who had not said a word in the entire meeting, piped up and reminded the brothers that last year each brother netted over $480,000 from Koch Soda. While it is true that things needed to get better with union wages and shrinking market share, she could not see $480,000 of income as being at the panic-triggering level.

Trudy explained that the expanding sports drink market was the main reason for Koch Soda market share reduction; union costs contributed a minor amount to slowing sales. Luke suggested they diversify their product line to include more "health drinks." The Koch brothers instantaneously responded with unmitigated absolute unwavering certainty, stating in operatic unison "we have no choice but to close this factory." Being certain and being wrong are frequently close partners, I think.

After long discussions with Koch fruit juicing people, Luke arrived at a very reasonable price for Koch doing the squeezing of lemons into juice. They had to drop the price, since the soon-to-be-defunct Koch Soda canning factory was removing 40% of their revenue. With the demand for squeezing down, Luke got a squeezing price break. Yes, Luke was happy with the price for squeezing, and was equally glad he got to know the Koch brothers. They were like all of us, a mix of both good and bad. But with patience and lots of rational thinking, we found a way to build a good win/win relationship.

CONCEPTUAL VALUE CHAIN MODEL

On the next page is the conceptual value chain model for Luke's Lemons, Season #3, and below is a description of each of the actions.

1. Each Monday morning, Luke contacts the baseball stadium and the fairgrounds to determine how many lemonade six-packs they will need for the following Monday. This gives him a full week to prepare all the lemonade. The baseball stadium and the fairgrounds pay Luke in advance for the number of six-packs they will be getting the next week.
2. Luke adds up the six-packs for the baseball stadium and the fairgrounds. Then he translates the total needed into how many bushels of lemons are needed. Luke tells Jose and Manuel how many bushels to pick. Jose and Manuel are paid for the picking in advance of them actually doing the work.
3. Jose and Manuel pick the proper number of bushels of lemons.
4. They transport the lemons to the Koch Juicer building.

Luke's Lemons- Conceptual DFD- Season #3

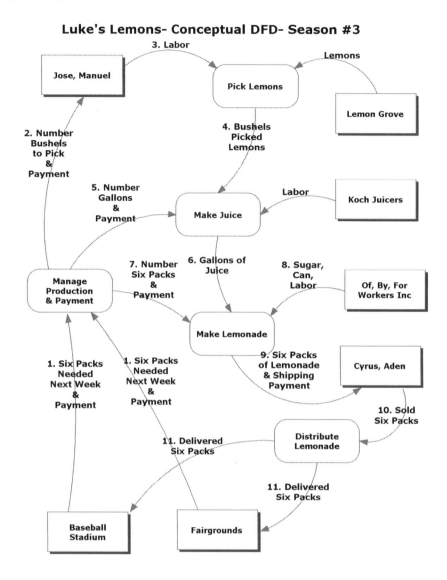

5. Luke tells the Koch Juicer manager how many gallons of juice are needed for next Monday's delivery. Luke pays Koch for the juice in advance. The lemons are squeezed and the juice bottled into the proper number of gallons.

6. The gallons of juice are transported by Koch to the company Of, By, & For the Workers, Inc.

7. Luke tells the manager at Of, By, & For the Workers, Inc. how many six-packs of lemonade are needed. Luke pays them in advance for both the six-packs and for the shipping.

8. Of, By, & For the Workers, Inc. takes the juice and adds water and sugar, and then cans the lemon juice to make lemonade. The cans are connected into six-packs by a machine.

9. The six-packs are transported to Cyrus and Aden. Cyrus and Aden are paid in advance for their distribution work.
10. Cyrus and Aden separate the six-packs into the proper quantities for each customer.
11. Cyrus delivers six-packs to the baseball stadium. Aden delivers six-packs to the fairgrounds.

CONCEPTUAL DATA MODEL

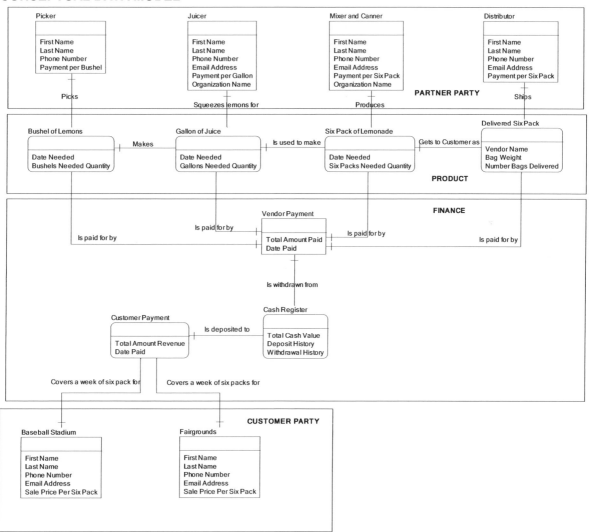

Here is a description of each of the relationships:

- A picker picks lemons to fill a bushel basket.
- A juicer squeezes lemons to make a gallon of juice.

- A mixer and canner produces a six-pack of lemonade by mixing juice, water, and sugar; sealing it into a can; and then attaches six cans into a single package.
- A distributor sorts the six-packs into quantities for each customer and then delivers the appropriate quantity to each customer.
- A bushel of lemons is paid for by a vendor payment made in advance of the lemons being picked.
- A gallon of juice is paid for by a vendor payment made in advance of the juice being made.
- A six-pack of lemonade is paid for by a vendor payment that is made in advance of the six-packs being made.
- A delivered six-pack is paid for by a vendor payment and is made in advance of the shipping of the six-packs.
- Each vendor payment is withdrawn from the cash register.
- Each customer payment for six-packs of lemonade is deposited to the cash register.
- Each customer payment covers a week of lemonade for the baseball stadium.
- Each customer payment covers a week of lemonade for the fairgrounds.

Here is a description of each of the entities, grouped by subject area:

- Party
  - **Picker**–the people who use ladders to pick the lemons from the trees and place them in bushel baskets.
  - **Juicer**–the people who squeeze the lemons to make lemon juice.
  - **Mixer and Canner**–the people who mix lemon juice, water, and sugar and seal it into cans to make lemonade. The cans are grouped into six-packs.
  - **Distributor**–the people who deliver six-packs of lemonade to the customers.
  - **Baseball Stadium**–the people who sell refreshments to the audience at baseball games.
  - **Fairgrounds**–the people who sell refreshments to attendees at the fairground events.
- Product
  - **Bushel of Lemons**–a basket filled with lemons. Each bushel holds about 500 lemons.
  - **Gallon of Juice**–a jar of lemon juice. Each bushel makes about two gallons of juice.
  - **Six-pack of Lemonade**–six cans of lemonade attached in a single package. Each gallon of juice makes about 3 six-packs.
  - **Delivered Six-pack**–the customer's quantities of six-packs sitting on their loading dock.

- Finance
  - **Vendor Payment**–a record of when and how much Luke's Lemons has paid to each vendor to cover the work they performed in the lemonade business.
  - **Cash Register**–the place where funds are stored.
  - **Customer Payment**–a record of when and how much each customer has paid to Luke's Lemons in exchange for lemonade.

LOGICAL VALUE CHAIN MODEL

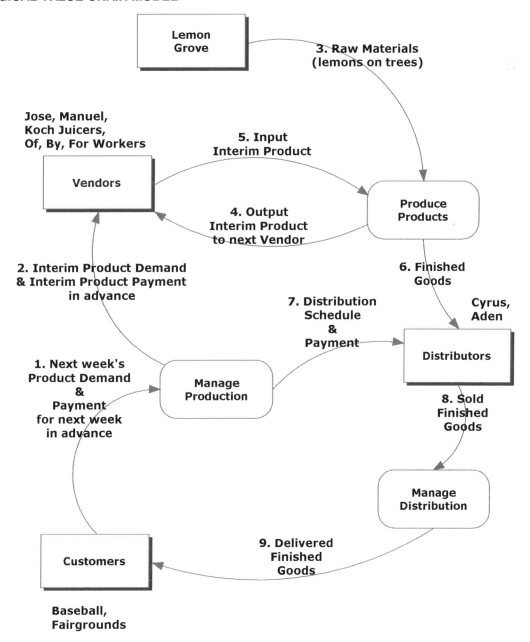

LOGICAL DATA MODEL

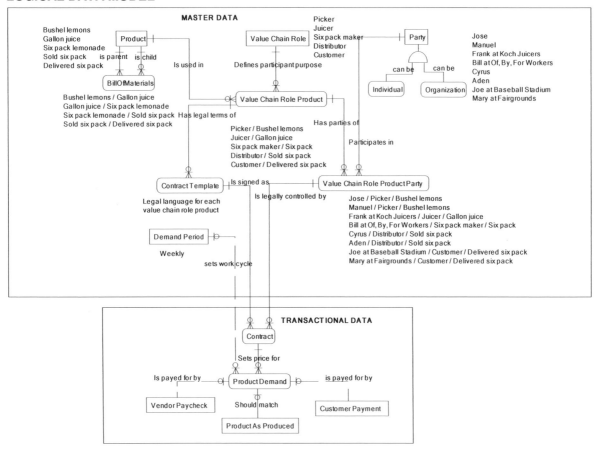

Here is a description of each of the relationships:

- A party cannot be both an individual and an organization. A party can be just an individual, or it can be just an organization.
- A value chain role defines each participant's purpose when dealing with a product.
- A product can be a parent in the bill of materials.
- A product can be a child in the bill of materials.
- A product is used in a value chain role product.
- Each value chain role product has legal terms and conditions stored in a contract template.
- Each value chain role product has parties associated in the value chain role product party.
- Each contract template is copied and signed to become a contract.
- Each value chain role product party has behavior controlled by the legal terms of the contract.
- Each contract sets the price for products as demanded each week by the customer.

- Each demand period defines the interval for forecasting and delivery of products.
- The production costs of product demand are paid for by the vendor paycheck.
- The consumer revenue generated by product demand is paid for by the customer payment.
- The product as produced should match the product demand. If the product demand does not match the product as produced and delivered, then a credit or debit adjustment will be issued at the end of the summer to each party.

Here is a description of each of the master data entities, grouped by subject area:

Product
  - **Product**–the finished goods or the interim product or the raw materials. Finished goods are six-packs of lemonade, Interim products are bushels of lemons, gallons of juice and Raw material products are lemons on trees.
  - **Bill of Materials**–the assembly structure to get from raw materials to interim products to finished goods.

Party
  - **Party**–the collection of people and organizations involved in Luke's Lemons, Inc.
  - **Individual**–the people involved in Luke's Lemons, Inc.
  - **Organization**–the legal business entities involved in Luke's Lemons, Inc.

Value Chain Design
  - **Value Chain Role**–the purpose of each party in Luke's Lemons, Inc.
  - **Value Chain Role Product**–the products delivered by each value chain role.
  - **Value Chain Role Product Party**–the parties who will execute a value chain role to product a product.
  - **Contract Template**–the legal language constraining behavior for each value chain role and the product it will produce.
  - **Demand Period**–the interval for which product demand will be forecast and the interval for product delivery to customer.

Here is a description of each of the transactional data entities:

  - **Contract**–an instance of a contract template that constrains the behavior of all parties in the lemonade value chain.
  - **Product Demand**–a forecast of how much lemonade a customer will need for a given demand period or a request for a partner party to produce bushels of lemons, gallons of juice, or six-packs of lemonade for a given demand period.
  - **Vendor Paycheck**–the payment to parties who contributed value in the lemonade value chain.

- **Customer Payment**–revenue collected by Luke's Lemons, Inc. in exchange for lemonade to be delivered to the customer.
- **Product as Produced**–the actual number of six-packs delivered to meet the product demand the customer gave us a week prior. If the demanded product and the produced product quantities are different, adjustments will be made to compensate for the difference.

Business Intelligence

Business intelligence data is created by transforming the master data and transactional data into a star schema. Star schemas have a fact table that is the finest granularity of metric in the design, and the fact table has various dimensions that serve as aggregation criteria for the facts. On the facing page is a star schema transformed from the Season #3 LDM.

We can mix and match dimensions to create thousands of queries on the star schema. Below are just a few of the queries that are possible:

- For the month of July, for Bushels of lemons, sum the payments
- For the month of July, for Bushels of lemons, sum the payments and divide the total July revenue by the sum of payments for Bushels of lemons for July
- For Manuel, sum payments
- For Customer of Mary Short / Fairgrounds, for July, sum the revenue

The progress in Luke's business over three summers was truly gratifying for all of the participants. He had grown from a mischievous little boy into a confident, mischievous big boy. This sounds like a small change, but a sense of self-confidence is the basis for forgiving and compromise. Cyrus and Aden had both experienced similar maturity, as their families were proud to testify.

The only bump in the road this season came towards the end of the summer when we were running out of lemons. The baseball team was in the playoffs, and the boys could see that they would be completely out of lemons sometime during the playoffs. This crisis precipitated a partnership with our neighbor Hank, who has seven acres of lemon trees. We added Hank and his kids to our value chain process at the last minute and ended up serving lemonade all through the sold-out playoffs. With the computing system and processes built around value chain and data models, the addition of our neighbors to the process and system was easy and fast, as planned.

Measurement Data

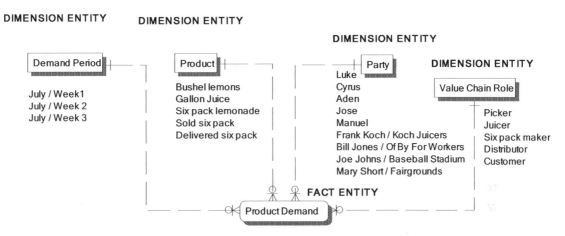

July / Week1 / Bushel lemons / Jose / Picker / 44 bushels / paid $80
July / Week1 / Bushel lemons / Manuel / Picker / 8 bushels / paid $20
July / Week1 / Gallon juice / Frank Koch / Koch Juicers / Juicer / 80 gallons / paid $75
July / Week1 / Six pack lemonade / Bill Jones / Of By For Workers / Six pack maker / 155 six packs / paid $65
July / Week1 / Sold six pack / Cyrus / Distributor / 70 six packs / paid $40
July / Week1 / Sold six pack / Aden / Distributor / 85 six packs / paid $49

July / Week1 / Delivered six pack / Joe Johns / Baseball Stadium / Customer / 70 six packs / collected $300
July / Week1 / Delivered six pack / Mary Short / Fairgrounds / Customer / 85 six packs / collected $342

QUERIES:
For Week1, sum payments and sum collections

For Week1, subtract payments sum from collections sum

RESULTS:
Week1 / paid = $329
Week1 / collected = $642

Week1 / profit = $313

The boys raked in about $9,900.00 each, leaving the business with $4,200.00 cash on hand. As in previous summers, all the participants in Luke's business had a clear understanding of how the value chain worked and used vocabulary from the data model in their conversations about the business. The computing system reinforced the vocabulary and flow in the value chain. We attributed much of our success to blind luck. The weather, the baseball team, the cheap picking labor, and a host of other lucky factors all just seemed to align for success. At the same time, I must say that Luke had a paradigm for how to approach his business that helped him to organize, structure, and orchestrate the pieces that accidentally fell his way. Once again, structure and creativity team up to generate synergy and success.

Data Model for Data Modeling and Value Chain

Below is a conceptual data model describing the entities and relationship involved in the CDM, LDM, conceptual value chain processes, and logical value chain process.

The transformation entities represent the engineering process that changes the CDM into the LDM for forward engineering and changes the LDM into the CDM for reverse engineering.

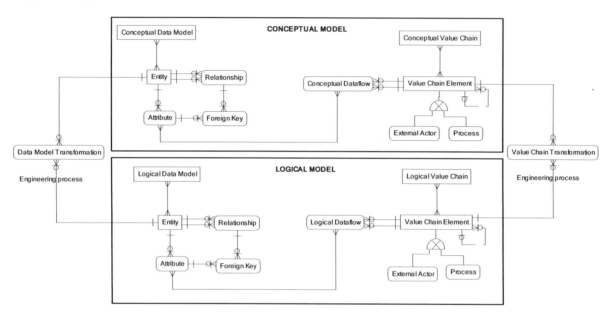

Forward Engineering the To-Be Business and System

Forward engineering is used to define a new and better way to operate your business and your computing systems. Forward engineering is a top-down process that starts with business experts envisioning a better tomorrow, then:

- A scope statement is formulated for the new project.
- Conceptual data models and value chains are designed.
- Logical data models and value chains are designed.
- Physical data models and value chains are designed.
- New human and machine physical instructions are built, tested, and deployed.
- The project operates as part of the real world.

The top-down design of tomorrow's world is called the to-be design.

Reverse Engineering the As-Is Business and System

Reverse engineering is a bit of a misnomer. John Zachman once said you cannot reverse engineer something that was not engineered when it was designed and built. A better phrase would be "documenting what you have today." An example, bottom-up, documenting what you have today:

- The executable computing system components are documented by the source code
- Database source code can be documented by physical data model graphic and text
- Physical database diagrams can be documented by logical model graphic and text
- Logical data model diagrams can be documented by conceptual model graphic and text
- Conceptual data model diagrams can be placed in a context with a statement of scope

Fast Forward

Luke's summer lemon business continued to evolve over the years. He eventually took over the computing system that ran his business. I would review his software designs, but he, Cyrus, and Aden did all the coding and testing. The early seasons when profitability spiked were never duplicated. The businesses profits flattened out for several years, although the boys were still making good money for a summer job.

BOY SCOUTS
I forced Luke to participate in Boy Scouts starting in fifth grade. It was the standard story; complain for a few months and then enjoy the next seven years. Since Cyrus and Aden joined the same troop, it made it easier for Luke to hike through the woods, sleep on the ground, and struggle with the vicissitudes of nature. Luke never grew to fully enjoy camping, but he learned many valuable lessons from scouting.

JOB BEFORE COLLEGE
After Luke graduated from high school, he decided to work for a couple of years before starting college. I went from high school straight to college in 1967. As a student and touring rock guitar player, my college grades might have suffered more than my pride can discuss at this time. I was glad to hear Luke would start college with full time work experiences in his bag of tricks.

Final Lesson

Before Luke took off for college, I offered one final lesson on the whiteboard. He was in the process of declining when he abruptly stopped and said "Sure, one last lesson would be okay." I knew he wanted to take his latest girlfriend to the movies that night, so I kept the lesson under 15 minutes.

We had bought the whiteboard when he was three; now he was getting one last lesson before launching off to college. I asked what topic he would like, and he picked "diversity and unity." He clarified that his interest was in knowing how things are both "separate and unique" and "not separate and not unique."

"Luke," I said, "do you remember the data model and value chain model you made when you were 10 years old? Here is what it looks like from the viewpoint of diversity. All entities are separate and unique." During our early tries at these designs, we laid out the things and talked about them before we created the relationships between things. On the facing page is an early version of Luke's models for Season #1.

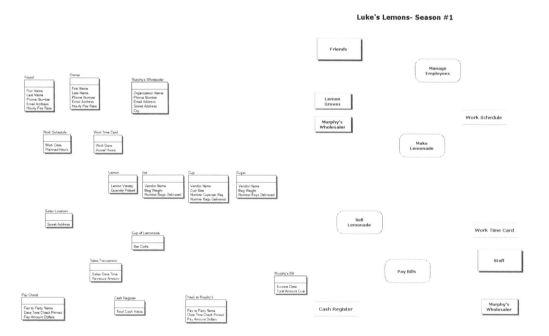

Luke's Lemons- Season #1

Next, I found our completed models with the relationships present. This web of formerly separate things is unity. If you grab one thing below and shake it, then entire web of related things will shake as well. Remember the spider webs that shook in unison? This is unity.

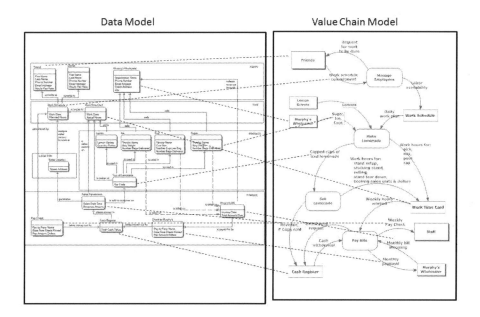

To answer Luke's specific question about how things are both separate and not separate, I replied that <u>things are not separate</u>. We trick ourselves into seeing things as separate, but this illusion exists because our brains perceive a <u>small slice of the real world</u>.

When we started our design for the first season, we had separate boxes in our diagrams. We were seeing a simplification (small slice) of the complexity of the real world. Later, when we were ready to address more complexity, we started to weave a web from separate things. We added the flows in the value chain. We added the relationships to the data model. We added dashed lines to relate the data to the flow. With all interdependencies identified, we understood the full reality and meaning of the first summer in the lemon business.

Luke decided to major in computer science to follow in dad's footsteps. In his first year of college he returned home for Thanksgiving holiday with lots of energy for his schoolwork and some frustration on one particular project. Luke was in the middle of a group project to build software to perform student billing at his college. The best team project would be given to the college information technology group to be incorporated into the billing system used by the college. Luke expressed frustration that his team was not functioning well. Luke's team was called The Sprinters and was composed of four people. Luke and Sue got along well and Tom and Terry got along well, but the team could not operate as a whole.

Luke and Sue were both politically liberal and thrived on adventure and spontaneity. Tom and Terry were both politically conservative and preferred low risk well planned activities. Luke was desperate to break the team log-jam that blocked consensus. I tried to explain what was happening to The Sprinters:

Our brains are the byproduct of millions of years of evolution. Our ancestors spent millions of years below the top of the food chain, so they had to observe the world and react with clear and decisive actions in a matter of seconds. Failure to do this could result in being eaten alive. We have a primitive part of our brains and a modern part of our brains. The primitive intuitive part of our brain is 99% of the neurons and the modern rational part is 1%. The primitive part of our brain is responsible for quickly identifying things like friends versus foes and good versus bad. The primitive brain generates lightning quick intuitions that are laced with complete certainty. This optimized survival for our ancestors, although it may spell disaster for modern mankind. After the primitive brain formulates an intuition, our modern brain searches for after-the-fact evidence to support our hastily formed intuitions.

One function of our primitive intuitive brain is to identify the object in our field of view as well as to identify the context or background for the object. This is called "figure versus ground". The picture on the facing page is ambiguous about figure versus ground. Some people see two faces and other people see one vase. Our intuitive brain struggles to see that the picture can be accurately seen as two faces or a vase, and could also be seen as two faces between a vase. Our primitive intuitive brain cannot see both sides of reality easily and our modern brain (1% of the neurons) is hesitant to overrule our seemingly bulletproof intuitions.

Luke, you have a team with two factions that see the world differently:

Point number one is do not appeal to the logic and rationality of Tom and Terry's modern brain. Explaining why teamwork is good with evidence and logic is not effective with the primitive brain (99% of the neurons).

Point number two is to appeal to the primitive part of Tom and Terry's brains. This is best done by getting to know them outside of the classroom project. Do not discuss the project as you meet socially. Prepare yourself to not discuss politics, religion or any other controversial topic during your get-to-know-you social events. Learn about Tom and Terry's hopes, dreams, hobbies, families, strengths and weaknesses. Share the same about yourself if the topic arises. Be sympathetic and genuinely compassionate towards them and over time a sense of trust will grow in everyone's primitive brains.

Point number three is that opposites are a necessary part of a strong whole. If the two faces in the picture above were gone, the vase would vanish. You must constantly be aware during your engagements with Tom and Terry that the universe created diversity because it is healthy and productive for individuals and for the species. When liberals and conservatives collaborate, listen and work toward a higher goal, then mountains can be moved.

Point number four is that we must cultivate humility since we need our opposites to be successful and we need to maintain a strong bridge of communication and collaboration with those who are our opposites.

Luke returned to school and implemented most of the four points. The Sprinters came in second place in the billing project competition and all four members received an A for their project grade.

Luke would continue to cultivate humility after college and took pride in the diversity and closeness of his group of friends. Today Luke appreciates face to face interaction with others, working in groups to achieve goals, respects the diverse views of others and has the skills for a happy and successful life.

Index

NOTE: **Bold** numbers indicate the pages where the term is defined.